PUBLIC AND PRIVATE SELF
IN
JAPAN AND THE UNITED
STATES

Communicative Styles of
Two Cultures

Dean C. Barnlund

INTERCULTURAL PRESS, INC.

PUBLIC AND PRIVATE SELF
IN
JAPAN AND THE UNITED STATES

PREFACE

An ancient image of broken communication—the Tower of Babel—seems far more appropriate to represent the plight of modern men than of men of earlier ages. People have always been plagued by a multiplicity of languages, but formerly most talking was confined to a local village where only the ordinary errors arising within a common dialect produced friction or misunderstanding. Each tribe talked mainly to itself. It is today, however, when people face each other daily across tribal, racial and religious boundaries that Babel seems to truly symbolize the human condition. It appears that men have never spoken in such a confusion of tongues. As we seek to find each other in a thicket of conflicting grammars—not just of words, but of gestures and vocal nuances—the risk of personal and national tragedy increases.

Nor is this sort of confusion confined any longer to encounters between nations. Differences often erupt dramatically within cultures as well. There is a growing appreciation that societies today are no longer single entities, but mosaics of distinctive and viable subcultures; old and young, male and female, rural and urban, rich and poor, cosmopolitan and provincial. Traffic is often as difficult and tenuous across these subcultural boundaries as across the borders of national states.

Another cultural divide has appeared in recent decades; it is the widening gap between specialists and nonspecialists. This is rightly of concern when it divides the physical scientist and the layman, but is of immensely more serious proportions when it isolates the behavioral scientist and layman. For the object of study of the behavioral scientist is human behavior: whatever discoveries he makes belong properly to all human beings. Yet these truths are often rendered inaccessible, locked inside an esoteric jargon that mystifies or frightens the nonspecialist. It is not surprising if in their discouragement ordinary people are forced to seek advice on interpersonal problems from popular magazines or collections of commonplaces. These momentarily dull the appetite without satisfying the deeper need to understand one's self and one's society. If specialists in human behavior cannot or do not speak in comprehensible terms, those without qualifications will not hesitate to do so.

This book is a preliminary report of studies investigating the character of interpersonal communication in Japan and the United States, with special emphasis upon the distinctiveness of Japanese patterns of interaction. Three aims guided the project: to develop a theoretical framework for examining differences in communicative behavior; to gather data on the actual conduct of face-to-face encounters in both countries; to speculate on the personal and social significance of differences in patterns of interacting. Thus the book opens by suggesting the growing importance of intercultural understanding, and by postulating a basic difference between Japanese and Americans with regard to their interpersonal accessibility. It develops the notion that the "public self" and "private self" bear unique relationships in these two countries, and discusses the consequences of this idea. Next, national differences in communicative patterns are examined in detail—what people prefer to talk about and avoid talking about, to whom they talk and do not talk, in what ways, verbal and nonverbal, they express themselves, and the defensive techniques they favor when placed in threatening interpersonal situations. The book concludes by commenting on relationships among the findings and speculating on the personal and social implications they may have. Thus it combines a broad profile of the dominant features of communication in these contrasting social systems with concrete details concerning the actual conduct of interpersonal affairs in Japan and the United States.

Underlying the entire work is the premise that the human personality and the social structure are interlocking systems. The individual and society are antecedent and consequent of each other: every person is at once a creator of society and its most obvious product. Individual acts are framed within a cultural imperative, but cultures derive their imperatives from the acts of individuals. Whether one begins his study of the human condition from the locus of society or of the individuals that comprise it, he ends by winding his way back to the same reality. Here the attempt is to assist in the comprehension of society by inspecting its most mundane and tangible acts—the messages people use to assert their identity and to bind them to the community of other human beings.

In form this book seeks to avoid being either a collection of speculations or a detailed summary of research data. It strives for some useful compromise between these extremes. Perhaps neither the generalist nor the specialist will approve entirely of this "arranged marriage" of writing styles, but it seemed the most fruitful way of sharing this experience. Where it appeared reasonable to generalize about the unique properties of communication in Japan or the United States, this has been done. Often, for the sake of clarity, statements are offered unencumbered by the situational qualifications that might influence their application in a specific setting.

Wherever appropriate, data are reported from a series of surveys carried out in Japan and the United States. These are intended to give substance and anchorage to generalizations about cultural characteristics. In some instances they illustrate, in others they document more rigorously, the conclusions that have been drawn. But they, too, are presented parsimoniously in the text, without resorting as in formal research to arrays of tables or elaborate descriptions of statistical tests. (The interest of the specialist is not disregarded; an appendix provides a summary of the raw data.) Throughout, the effort has been to blend fact and theory into a readable style without overwhelming the reader with indigestible detail or underwhelming him with groundless speculation.

There are two views of the scientific enterprise. One stresses the need for definitive studies. The scientist should work patiently, gradually accumulating data and subjecting them to every test, refusing to share the results until all the findings are in and every imperfection corrected. A second view regards research as a process, always incomplete, always clouded by errors, but with a growing residue of accomplishment. The first scientist regards his work as one might a formal document, aiming at the most perfect formulation of an idea in its final form. The second sees his research as part of a dialogue, a continuing, imprecise conversation, terminating periodically in moments of consensus. The content of this book reflects the latter view, and should be seen as no more than an opening remark in a continuing and fascinating exploration of cultural differences in communicative styles.

The risks that attend the comparative study of human cultures are both immense and unavoidable. The first, and most obvious, is that a society is a cumbersome and complicated specimen for scientific study. It does not hold still. It cannot be manipulated. Its elements are all unique. It is easy, therefore, to be overwhelmed by unmanageable detail. In seeking to render such detail more comprehensible by searching for underlying patterns and consistencies, there is always danger of oversimplification. Cultural generalizations, therefore, need to be viewed as approximations, not absolutes. Many readers will find occasions when specific acts of specific persons on specific occasions do not fit the descriptions given here. The issue, however, is not whether cultural generalizations account for every act of every person, but whether they help to explain the meaning of many or most social events.

The second risk seems equally unavoidable, and is even more capable of provoking misunderstanding. And, for someone who holds both of these cultures in deep respect, it is a particularly painful risk to assume. It arises from the difficulty of making any comparative statement without implying, or having attributed to it, some sort of cosmic judgment. No matter how careful the research, it must embody the assumptions of some culture; no matter how objective the conclusions, they must be stated and read from some cultural perspective. Although the effects of cultural biases can be resisted, they can never be totally eliminated. The best that can be done is to acknowledge this fact, and to encourage parallel studies that incorporate the biases of some other culture. It has been a source of some satisfaction that readers of this manuscript have felt the findings did describe and explain much of their own behavior and, at the same time, members of both cultures felt the account favored their own culture too much. Upon reflection this is not as surprising as it seems. Viewed from the perspective of two cultures that operate on such different, and in many respects opposite, assumptions should lead to contradictory evaluations of the same act.

This research on the communicative styles of Japanese and Americans was first published in Japanese by The Simul Press in 1973, under the title *Nipponjin no Hyogen Kozo* (Structure of Japanese Expression). It has been gratifying that the Japanese edition has been highly praised by Japanese specialists and the general public as well. In preparing this edition I have had an opportunity to give a fuller report of the findings and to extend the interpretations of these findings.

A publication of this kind seldom carries the sound of a single voice. More often it echoes a chorus of specialists, all of whom entered at some critical moment and contributed to the final product. There are many upon whose generosity, sensitivity, and insight the author has drawn. My good friends and colleagues, Dr. Mitsuko Saito Fukunaga and Dr. John Condon obtained financial support for my work, have encouraged and assisted me in many ways, and have been my professional companions in exploring intercultural differences. The Japan Society for the Promotion of Science, through its Visiting Scientists Program, enabled me to undertake research in Japan, and International Christian University has provided me with a position on two visits there.

A very critical role in formulating my own direction in these studies was played by the interdisciplinary seminars sponsored by the Japanese Ministry of Education. Through discussions with scholars such as Dr. Takeo Doi, Dr. Akira Hoshino, Dr. Tetsuya Kunihiro, Dr. Arimasa Mori, Dr. Chie Nakane, Dr. Linju Ogasawara, and the others who participated in these meetings, I gained incentive to continue my work and constructive suggestions as well. In the collection of data in the United States I had the generous assistance of Dr. Franklyn Haiman, Dr. Alvin Goldberg, Dr. Joel Litvin, Dr. David Seibert, James Ahern and Milton Bennett. Throughout the study I have benefited repeatedly from the liberal assistance and perceptive suggestions of Masako Sano. In the preparation of the Japanese and English editions of the manuscript I have enjoyed the unqualified support and generous assistance of Mr. Katsuo Tamura, President and Editor-in-Chief of The Simul Press, and of his talented and conscientious staff. His lively interest and personal warmth have made work on this project an unforeseen pleasure; I count our personal friendship among its most valued consequences. Finally, my deep appreciation to my students who have both stimulated and corrected me, often by the same remark. In many respects they have been my collaborators and tutors.

DEAN C. BARNLUND
San Francisco, 1975
(Tokyo, 1973)

CONTENTS

PUBLIC AND PRIVATE SELF
IN
JAPAN AND THE UNITED STATES

*I think there is nothing barbarous and savage ...
except that each man calls barbarism whatever is not
his own practice; for indeed it seems we have no other
test of truth and reason than the example and pattern
of the opinions and customs of the country we live in.*

... Montaigne

*Interaction lies at the hub of the universe of culture
and everything grows from it.*

... Edward Hall

1 | Communication in a Global Village

Nearing Autumn's close.
My neighbor—
How does he live, I wonder?   ...Bashō

These lines, written by one of the most cherished of *haiku* poets, express a timeless and universal curiosity in one's fellow man. When they were written, nearly three hundred years ago, the word "neighbor" referred to people very much like one's self— similar in dress, in diet, in custom, in language—who happened to live next door. Today relatively few people are surrounded by neighbors who are cultural replicas of themselves. Tomorrow we can expect to spend most of our lives in the company of neighbors who will speak in a different tongue, seek different values, move at a different pace, and interact according to a different script. Within no longer than a decade or two the probability of spending part of one's life in a foreign culture will exceed the probability a hundred years ago of ever leaving the town in which one was born. As our world is transformed our neighbors increasingly will be people whose life styles contrast sharply with our own.

The technological feasibility of such a global village is no longer in doubt. Only the precise date of its attainment is uncertain. The means already exist: in telecommunication systems linking the world by satellite, in aircraft capable of moving people faster than the speed of sound, in computers which can disgorge facts more rapidly than men can formulate their questions. The methods for bringing people closer physically and electronically are clearly at hand. What is in doubt is whether the erosion of cultural boundaries through technology will bring the realization of a dream or a nightmare. Will a global village be a mere collection or a true community of men? Will its residents be neighbors capable of respecting and utilizing their differences, or clusters of strangers living in ghettos and united only in their antipathies for others?

Can we generate the new cultural attitudes required by our technological virtuosity? History is not very reassuring here. It has taken centuries to learn how to live harmoniously in the family, the tribe, the city state, and the nation. Each new stretching of human sensitivity and loyalty has taken generations to become firmly assimilated in the human psyche. And now we are forced into a quantum leap from the mutual suspicion and hostility that have marked the past relations between peoples into a world in which mutual respect and comprehension are requisite.

Even events of recent decades provide little basis for optimism. Increasing physical proximity has brought no millenium in human relations. If anything, it has appeared to intensify the divisions among people rather than to create a broader intimacy. Every new reduction in physical distance has made us more painfully aware of the psychic distance that divides people and has increased alarm over real or imagined differences. If today people occasionally choke on what seem to be indigestible differences between rich and poor, male and female, specialist and nonspecialist within cultures, what will happen tomorrow when people must assimilate and cope with still greater contrasts in life styles? Wider access to more people will be a doubtful victory if human beings find they have nothing to say to one another or cannot stand to listen to each other.

Time and space have long cushioned intercultural encounters, confining them to touristic exchanges. But this insulation is rapidly wearing thin. In the world of tomorrow we can expect to live—not merely vacation—in societies which seek different values and abide by different codes. There we will be surrounded by foreigners for long periods of time, working with others in the closest possible relationships. If people currently show little tolerance or talent for encounters with alien cultures, how can they learn to deal with constant and inescapable coexistence?

The temptation is to retreat to some pious hope or talismanic formula to carry us into the new age. "Meanwhile," as Edwin Reischauer reminds us, "we fail to do what we ourselves must do if 'one world' is ever to be achieved, and that is to develop the education, the skills and the attitudes that men must have if they are to build and maintain such a world. The time is short, and the needs are great. The task faces all men. But it is on the shoulders of people living in the strong countries of the world, such as Japan and the United States, that this burden falls with special weight and urgency."[1]

Anyone who has truly struggled to comprehend another person —even those closest and most like himself—will appreciate the immensity of the challenge of intercultural communication. A greater exchange of people between nations, needed as that may be, carries with it no guarantee of increased cultural empathy; experience in other lands often does little but aggravate existing prejudices. Studying guidebooks or memorizing polite phrases similarly fails to explain differences in cultural perspectives. Programs of cultural enrichment, while they contribute to curiosity about other ways of life, do not cultivate the skills to function effectively in the cultures studied. Even concentrated exposure to a foreign language, valuable as it is, provides access to only one of the many codes that regulate daily affairs; human understanding is by no means guaranteed because conversants share the same dictionary. (Within the United States, where people inhabit a common territory and possess a common language, mutuality of meaning among Mexican-Americans, White-Americans, Black-Americans, Indian-Americans—to say nothing of old and young, poor and rich, pro-establishment and anti-establishment cultures —is a sporadic and unreliable occurrence.) Useful as all these measures are for enlarging appreciation of diverse cultures, they fall short of what is needed for a global village to survive.

What seems most critical is to find ways of gaining entrance into the assumptive world of another culture, to identify the norms that govern face-to-face relations, and to equip people to function within a social system that is foreign but no longer incomprehensible. Without this kind of insight people are condemned to remain outsiders no matter how long they live in another country. Its institutions and its customs will be interpreted inevitably from the premises and through the medium of their own culture. Whether they notice something or overlook it, respect or ridicule it, express or conceal their reaction will be dictated by the logic of their own rather than the alien culture.

There are, of course, shelves and shelves of books on the cultures of the world. They cover the history, religion, political thought, music, sculpture, and industry of many nations. And they make fascinating and provocative reading. But only in the vaguest way do they suggest what it is that really distinguishes the behavior of a Samoan, a Congolese, a Japanese or an American. Rarely do the descriptions of a political structure or religious faith explain precisely when and why certain topics are avoided or why specific gestures carry such radically different meanings according to the context in which they appear.

When former President Nixon and former Premier Sato met to discuss a growing problem concerning trade in textiles between Japan and the United States, Premier Sato announced that since they were on such good terms with each other that the deliberations would be "three parts talk and seven parts 'haragei'."[2] Translated literally, "haragei" means to communicate through the belly, that is to feel out intuitively rather than verbally state the precise position of each person.

Subscribing to this strategy—one that governs many interpersonal exchanges in his culture—Premier Sato conveyed without verbal elaboration his comprehension of the plight of American textile firms threatened by accelerating exports of Japanese fabrics to the United States. President Nixon—similarly abiding by norms that govern interaction within his culture—took this comprehension of the American position to mean that new export quotas would be forthcoming shortly.

During the next few weeks both were shocked at the consequences of their meeting: Nixon was infuriated to learn that the new policies he expected were not forthcoming, and Sato was upset to find that he had unwittingly triggered a new wave of hostility toward his country. If prominent officials, surrounded by foreign advisers, can commit such grievous communicative blunders, the plight of the ordinary citizen may be suggested. Such intercultural collisions, forced upon the public consciousness by the grave consequences they carry and the extensive publicity they receive, only hint at the wider and more frequent confusions and hostilities that disrupt the negotiations of lesser officials, business executives, professionals and even visitors in foreign countries.

Every culture expresses its purposes and conducts its affairs through the medium of communication. Cultures exist primarily to create and preserve common systems of symbols by which their members can assign and exchange meanings. Unhappily, the distinctive rules that govern these symbol systems are far from obvious. About some of these codes, such as language, we have extensive knowledge. About others, such as gestures and facial codes, we have only rudimentary knowledge. On many others— rules governing topical appropriateness, customs regulating physical contact, time and space codes, strategies for the management of conflict—we have almost no systematic knowledge. To crash another culture with only the vaguest notion of its underlying dynamics reflects not only a provincial naïvete but a dangerous form of cultural arrogance.

It is differences in meaning, far more than mere differences in vocabulary, that isolate cultures, and that cause them to regard each other as strange or even barbaric. It is not too surprising that many cultures refer to themselves as "The People," relegating all other human beings to a subhuman form of life. To the person who drinks blood, the eating of meat is repulsive. Someone who conveys respect by standing is upset by someone who conveys it by sitting down; both may regard kneeling as absurd. Burying the dead may prompt tears in one society, smiles in another, and dancing in a third. If spitting on the street makes sense to some, it will appear bizarre that others carry their spit in their pocket; neither may quite appreciate someone who spits to express gratitude. The bullfight that constitutes an almost religious ritual for some seems a cruel and inhumane way of destroying a defenseless animal to others. Although staring is acceptable social behavior in some cultures, in others it is a thoughtless invasion of privacy. Privacy, itself, is without universal meaning.

Note that none of these acts involves an insurmountable linguistic challenge. The words that describe these acts—eating, spitting, showing respect, fighting, burying, and staring—are quite translatable into most languages. The issue is more conceptual than linguistic; each society places events in its own cultural frame and it is these frames that bestow the unique meaning and differentiated response they produce.

As we move or are driven toward a global village and increasingly frequent cultural contact, we need more than simply greater factual knowledge of each other. We need, more specifically, to identify what might be called the "rulebooks of meaning" that distinguish one culture from another. For to grasp the way in which other cultures perceive the world, and the assumptions and values that are the foundation of these perceptions, is to gain access to the experience of other human beings. Access to the world view and the communicative style of other cultures may not only enlarge our own way of experiencing the world but enable us to maintain constructive relationships with societies that operate according to a different logic than our own.

Sources of Meaning

To survive, psychologically as well as physically, human beings must inhabit a world that is relatively free of ambiguity and reasonably predictable. Some sort of structure must be placed upon the endless profusion of incoming signals. The infant, born into a world of flashing, hissing, moving images soon learns to adapt by resolving this chaos into toys and tables, dogs and parents. Even adults who have had their vision or hearing restored through surgery describe the world as a frightening and sometimes unbearable experience; only after days of effort are they able to transform blurs and noises into meaningful and therefore manageable experiences.

It is commonplace to talk as if the world "has" meaning, to ask what "is" the meaning of a phrase, a gesture, a painting, a contract. Yet when thought about, it is clear that events are devoid of meaning until someone assigns it to them. There is no appropriate response to a bow or a handshake, a shout or a whisper, until it is interpreted. A drop of water and the color red have no meaning, they simply exist. The aim of human perception is to make the world intelligible so that it can be managed successfully; the attribution of meaning is a prerequisite to and preparation for action.[3]

People are never passive receivers, merely absorbing events of obvious significance, but are active in assigning meaning to sensation. What any event acquires in the way of meaning appears to reflect a transaction between what is there to be seen or heard, and what the interpreter brings to it in the way of past experience and prevailing motive. Thus the attribution of meaning is always a creative process by which the raw data of sensation are transformed to fit the aims of the observer.

The diversity of reactions that can be triggered by a single experience—meeting a stranger, negotiating a contract, attending a textile conference—is immense. Each observer is forced to see it through his own eyes, interpret it in the light of his own values, fit it to the requirements of his own circumstances. As a consequence, every object and message is seen by every observer from a somewhat different perspective. Each person will note some features and neglect others. Each will accept some relations among the facts and deny others. Each will arrive at some conclusion, tentative or certain, as the sounds and forms resolve into a "temple" or "barn," a "compliment" or "insult."

Provide a group of people with a set of photographs, even quite simple and ordinary photographs, and note how diverse are the meanings they provoke. Afterward they will recall and forget different pictures; they will also assign quite distinctive meanings to those they do remember. Some will recall the mood of a picture, others the actions; some the appearance and others the attitudes of persons portrayed. Often the observers cannot agree upon even the most "objective" details—the number of people, the precise location and identity of simple objects. A difference in frame of mind—fatigue, hunger, excitement, anger—will change dramatically what they report they have "seen."

It should not be surprising that people raised in different families, exposed to different events, praised and punished for different reasons, should come to view the world so differently. As George Kelly has noted, people see the world through templates which force them to construe events in unique ways. These patterns or grids which we fit over the realities of the world are cut from our own experience and values, and they predispose us to certain interpretations. Industrialist and farmer do not see the "same" land; husband and wife do not plan for the "same" child; doctor and patient do not discuss the "same" disease; borrower and creditor do not negotiate the "same" mortgage; daughter and daughter-in-law do not react to the "same" mother.

The world each person creates for himself is a distinctive world, not the same world others occupy. Each fashions from every incident whatever meanings fit his own private biases. These biases, taken together, constitute what has been called the "assumptive world of the individual." The world each person gets inside his head is the only world he knows. And it is this symbolic world, not the real world, that he talks about, argues about, laughs about, fights about.

Interpersonal Encounters

Every communication, interpersonal or intercultural, is a

transaction between these private worlds. As people talk they search for symbols that will enable them to share their experience and converge upon a common meaning. This process, often long and sometimes painful, makes it possible finally to reconcile apparent or real differences between them. Various words are used to describe this moment. When it involves an integration of facts or ideas, it is usually called an "agreement"; when it involves sharing a mood or feeling, it is referred to as "empathy" or "rapport." But "understanding" is a broad enough term to cover both possibilities; in either case it identifies the achievement of a common meaning.

If understanding is a measure of communicative success, a simple formula—which might be called the *Interpersonal Equation*—may clarify the major factors that contribute to its achievement:

Interpersonal Understanding = f (Similarity of Perceptual Orientations, Similarity of Belief Systems, Similarity of Communicative Styles)

That is, "Interpersonal Understanding" is a function of or dependent upon the degree of "Similarity of Perceptual Orientations," "Similarity of Systems of Belief," and "Similarity in Communicative Styles." Each of these terms requires some elaboration.

"Similarity in Perceptual Orientations" refers to a person's prevailing approach to reality and the degree of flexibility he manifests in organizing it. Some people scan the world broadly, searching for diversity of experience, preferring the novel and unpredictable. They may be drawn to new foods, new music, new ways of thinking. Others seem to scan the world more narrowly, searching to confirm past experience, preferring the known and predictable. They secure satisfaction from old friends, traditional art forms, familiar life styles. The former have a high tolerance for novelty; the latter a low tolerance for novelty.

It is a balance between these tendencies, of course, that characterizes most people. Within the same person attraction to the unfamiliar and the familiar coexist. Which prevails at any moment is at least partly a matter of circumstance: when secure, people may widen their perceptual field, accommodate new ideas or actions; when they feel insecure they may narrow their perceptual field to protect existing assumptions from the threat of new beliefs or life styles. The balance may be struck in still other ways: some people like to live in a stable physical setting with everything in its proper place, but welcome new emotional or intellectual challenges; others enjoy living in a chaotic and disordered environment but would rather avoid exposing themselves to novel or challenging ideas.

People differ also in the degree to which their perceptions are flexible or rigid. Some react with curiosity and delight to unpredictable and uncategorizable events. Others are disturbed or uncomfortable in the presence of the confusing and complex. There are people who show a high degree of tolerance for ambiguity; others manifest a low tolerance for ambiguity. When confronted with the complications and confusions that surround many daily events, the former tend to avoid immediate closure and delay judgment while the latter seek immediate closure and evaluation. Those with little tolerance for ambiguity tend to respond categorically, that is, by reference to the class names for things (businessmen, radicals, hippies, foreigners) rather than to their unique and differentiating features.

It would be reasonable to expect that individuals who approach reality similarly might understand each other easily, and laboratory research confirms this conclusion: people with similar perceptual styles attract one another, understand each other better, work more efficiently together and with greater satisfaction than those whose perceptual orientations differ.

"Similarity in Systems of Belief" refers not to the way people view the world, but to the conclusions they draw from their experience. Everyone develops a variety of opinions toward divorce, poverty, religion, television, sex, and social customs. When belief and disbelief systems coincide, people are likely to understand and appreciate each other better. Research done by Donn Byrne and replicated by the author demonstrates how powerfully human beings are drawn to those who hold the same beliefs and how sharply they are repelled by those who do not.[4]

Subjects in these experiments were given questionnaires requesting their opinions on twenty-six topics. After completing the forms, each was asked to rank the thirteen most important and least important topics. Later each person was given four forms, ostensibly filled out by people in another group but actually filled out to show varying degrees of agreement with their own answers, and invited to choose among them with regard to their attractiveness as associates. The results were clear: people most preferred to talk with those whose attitudes duplicated their own exactly, next chose those who agreed with them on all important issues, next chose those with similar views on unimportant issues, and finally and reluctantly chose those who disagreed with them completely. It appears that most people most of the time find satisfying relationships easiest to achieve with someone who shares their own hierarchy of beliefs. This, of course, converts many human encounters into rituals of ratification, each person looking to the other only to obtain endorsement and applause for his own beliefs. It is, however, what is often meant by "interpersonal understanding."

Does the same principle hold true for "Similarity of Communicative Styles?" To a large extent, yes. But not completely. By "communicative style" is meant the topics people prefer to discuss, their favorite forms of interaction—ritual, repartee, argument, self-disclosure—and the depth of involvement they demand of each other. It includes the extent to which communicants rely upon the same channels—vocal, verbal, physical—for conveying information, and the extent to which they are tuned to the same level of meaning, that is, to the factual or emotional content of messages. The use of a common vocabulary and even preference for similar metaphors may help people to understand each other.

But some complementarity in conversational style may also help. Talkative people may prefer quiet partners, the more aggressive may enjoy the less aggressive, those who seek affection may be drawn to the more affection-giving, simply because both can find the greatest mutual satisfaction when interpersonal styles mesh. Even this sort of complementarity, however, may reflect a case of similarity in definitions of each other's conversational role.

This hypothesis, too, has drawn the interest of communicologists. One investigator found that people paired to work on common tasks were much more effective if their communicative styles were similar than if they were dissimilar.[5] Another social scientist found that teachers tended to give higher grades on tests to students whose verbal styles matched their own than to students who gave equally valid answers but did not phrase them as their instructors might.[6] To establish common meanings seems to require that conversants share a common vocabulary and compatible ways of expressing ideas and feelings.

It must be emphasized that perceptual orientations, systems of belief, and communicative styles do not exist or operate independently. They overlap and affect each other. They combine in complex ways to determine behavior. What a person says is influenced by what he believes and what he believes, in turn, by what he sees. His perceptions and beliefs are themselves partly a product of his manner of communicating with others. The terms that comprise the Interpersonal Equation constitute not three isolated but three interdependent variables. They provide three perspectives to use in the analysis of communicative acts.

The Interpersonal Equation suggests there is an underlying narcissistic bias in human societies that draws similar people together. Each seeks to find in the other a reflection of himself, someone who views the world as he does, who interprets it as he does, and who expresses himself in a similar way. It is not surprising, then, that artists should be drawn to artists, radicals to radicals, Jews to Jews—or Japanese to Japanese and Americans to Americans.

The opposite seems equally true: people tend to avoid those who challenge their assumptions, who dismiss their beliefs, and who communicate in strange and unintelligible ways. When one reviews history, whether he examines crises within or between cultures, he finds people have consistently shielded themselves, segregated themselves, even fortified themselves, against wide differences in modes of perception or expression. (In many cases, indeed, have persecuted and conquered the infidel and afterwards substituted their own cultural ways for the offending ones.) Intercultural defensiveness appears to be only a counterpart of interpersonal defensiveness in the face of uncomprehended or incomprehensible differences.

Intercultural Encounters

Every culture attempts to create a "universe of discourse" for its members, a way in which people can interpret their experience and convey it to one another. Without a common system of codifying sensations, life would be absurd and all efforts to share

16

meanings doomed to failure. This universe of discourse—one of the most precious of all cultural legacies—is transmitted to each generation in part consciously and in part unconsciously. Parents and teachers give explicit instruction in it by praising or criticizing certain ways of dressing, of thinking, of gesturing, of responding to the acts of others. But the most significant aspects of any cultural code may be conveyed implicitly, not by rule or lesson but through modelling behavior. The child is surrounded by others who, through the mere consistency of their actions as males and females, mothers and fathers, salesclerks and policemen, display what is appropriate behavior. Thus the grammar of any culture is sent and received largely unconsciously, making one's own cultural assumptions and biases difficult to recognize. They seem so obviously right that they require no explanation.

In *The Open and Closed Mind*, Milton Rokeach poses the problem of cultural understanding in its simplest form, but one that can readily demonstrate the complications of communication between cultures. It is called the "Denny Doodlebug Problem." Readers are given all the rules that govern his culture: Denny is an animal that always faces North, and can move only by jumping; he can jump large distances or small distances, but can change direction only after jumping four times in any direction; he can jump North, South, East or West, but not diagonally. Upon concluding a jump his master places some food three feet directly West of him. Surveying the situation, Denny concludes he must jump four times to reach the food. No more or less. And he is right. All the reader has to do is to explain the circumstances that make his conclusion correct.[7]

The large majority of people who attempt this problem fail to solve it, despite the fact that they are given all the rules that control behavior in this culture. If there is difficulty in getting inside the simplistic world of Denny Doodlebug—where the cultural code has already been broken and handed to us—imagine the complexity of comprehending behavior in societies whose codes have not yet been deciphered. And where even those who obey these codes are only vaguely aware and can rarely describe the underlying sources of their own actions.

If two people, both of whom spring from a single culture, must often shout to be heard across the void that separates their private worlds, one can begin to appreciate the distance to be overcome when people of different cultural identities attempt to talk. Even with the most patient dedication to seeking a common terminology, it is surprising that people of alien cultures are able to hear each other at all. And the peoples of Japan and the United States would appear to constitute a particularly dramatic test of the ability to cross an intercultural divide. Consider the disparity between them.

Here is Japan, a tiny island nation with a minimum of resources, buffeted by periodic disasters, overcrowded with people, isolated by physical fact and cultural choice, nurtured in Shinto and Buddhist religions, permeated by a deep respect for nature, nonmaterialist in philosophy, intuitive in thought, hierarchical in social structure. Eschewing the explicit, the monumental, the bold and boisterous, it expresses its sensuality in the form of impeccable gardens, simple rural temples, asymmetrical flower arrangements, a theatre unparalleled for containment of feeling, an art and literature remarkable for their delicacy, and crafts noted for their honest and earthy character. Its people, among the most homogeneous of men, are modest and apologetic in manner, communicate in an ambiguous and evocative language, are engrossed in interpersonal rituals and prefer inner serenity to influencing others. They occupy unpretentious buildings of wood and paper and live in cities laid out as casually as farm villages. Suddenly from these rice paddies emerges an industrial giant, surpassing rival nations with decades of industrial experience, greater resources, and a larger reserve of technicians. Its labor, working longer, harder, and more frantically than any in the world, builds the earth's largest city, constructs some of its ugliest buildings, promotes the most garish and insistent advertising anywhere, and pollutes its air and water beyond the imagination.

And here is the United States, an immense country, sparsely settled, richly endowed, tied through waves of immigrants to the heritage of Europe, yet forced to subdue nature and find fresh solutions to the problems of survival. Steeped in the Judeo-Christian tradition, schooled in European abstract and analytic thought, it is materialist and experimental in outlook, philosophically pragmatic, politically equalitarian, economically competitive, its raw individualism sometimes tempered by a humanitarian concern for others. Its cities are studies in geometry along whose avenues rise shafts of steel and glass subdivided into separate cubicles for separate activities and separate people. Its popular arts are characterized by the hugeness of Cinemascope, the spontaneity of jazz, the earthy loudness of rock; in its fine arts the experimental, striking and monumental often stifle the more subtle revelation. The people, a smorgasbord of races, religions, dialects and nationalities, are turned expressively outward, impatient with rituals and rules, casual and flippant, gifted in logic and argument, approachable and direct yet given to flamboyant and exaggerated assertion. They are curious about one another, open and helpful, yet display a missionary zeal for changing one another. Suddenly this nation whose power and confidence have placed it in a dominant position in the world intellectually and politically, whose style of life has permeated the planet, finds itself uncertain of its direction, doubts its own premises and values, questions its motives and materialism, and engages in an orgy of self criticism.

It is when people nurtured in such different psychological worlds meet that differences in cultural perspectives and communicative codes may sabotage efforts to understand one another. Repeated collisions between a foreigner and the members of a contrasting culture often produce what is called "culture shock." It is a feeling of helplessness, even of terror or anger, that accompanies working in an alien society. One feels trapped in an absurd and indecipherable nightmare.

It is as if some hostile leprechaun had gotten into the works and as a cosmic caper rewired the connections that hold society together. Not only do the actions of others no longer make sense, but it is impossible even to express one's own intentions clearly. "Yes" comes out meaning "No." A wave of the hand means "come," or it may mean "go." Formality may be regarded as childish, or as a devious form of flattery. Statements of fact may be heard as statements of conceit. Arriving early, or arriving late, embarrasses or impresses. "Suggestions" may be treated as "ultimatums," or precisely the opposite. Failure to stand at the proper moment, or failure to sit, may be insulting. The compliment intended to express gratitude instead conveys a sense of distance. A smile signifies disappointment rather than pleasure.

If the crises that follow such intercultural encounters are sufficiently dramatic or the communicants unusually sensitive, they may recognize the source of their trouble. If there is patience and constructive intention the confusion can sometimes be clarified. But more often the foreigner, without knowing it, leaves behind him a trail of frustration, mistrust, and even hatred *of which he is totally unaware*. Neither he nor his associates recognize that their difficulty springs from sources deep within the rhetoric of their own societies. Each sees himself as acting in ways that are thoroughly sensible, honest and considerate. And—given the rules governing his own universe of discourse—each is. Unfortunately, there are few cultural universals, and the degree of overlap in communicative codes is always less than perfect. Experience can be transmitted with fidelity only when the unique properties of each code are recognized and respected, or where the motivation and means exist to bring them into some sort of alignment.

The Collective Unconscious

Among the greatest insights of this modern age are two that bear a curious affinity to each other. The first, evolving from the efforts of psychologists, particularly Sigmund Freud, revealed the existence of an "individual unconscious." The acts of human beings were found to spring from motives of which they were often vaguely or completely unaware. Their unique perceptions of events arose not from the facts outside their skins but from unrecognized assumptions inside them. When, through intensive analysis, they obtained some insight into these assumptions, they became free to develop other ways of seeing and acting which contributed to their greater flexibility in coping with reality.

The second of these generative ideas, flowing from the work of anthropologists, particularly Margaret Mead and Ruth Benedict, postulated a parallel idea in the existence of a "cultural unconscious." Students of primitive cultures began to see that there was nothing divine or absolute about cultural norms. Every society had its own way of viewing the universe, and each developed from its premises a coherent set of rules of behavior. Each tended to be blindly committed to its own style of life and regarded all others as evil. The fortunate person who was able to master the art of living in foreign cultures often learned that his own mode of life was only one among many. With this insight he became free to choose from among cultural values those that seemed to best fit his peculiar circumstances.

Cultural norms so completely surround people, so permeate

thought and action, that few ever recognize the assumptions on which their lives and their sanity rest. As one observer put it, if birds were suddenly endowed with scientific curiosity they might examine many things, but the sky itself would be overlooked as a suitable subject; if fish were to become curious about the world, it would never occur to them to begin by investigating water. For birds and fish would take the sky and sea for granted, unaware of their profound influence because they comprise the medium for every act. Human beings, in a similar way, occupy a symbolic universe governed by codes that are unconsciously acquired and automatically employed. So much so that they rarely notice that the ways they interpret and talk about events are distinctively different from the ways people conduct their affairs in other cultures.

As long as people remain blind to the sources of their meanings, they are imprisoned within them. These cultural frames of reference are no less confining simply because they cannot be seen or touched. Whether it is an individual neurosis that keeps an individual out of contact with his neighbors, or a collective neurosis that separates neighbors of different cultures, both are forms of blindness that limit what can be experienced and what can be learned from others.

It would seem that everywhere people would desire to break out of the boundaries of their own experiential worlds. Their ability to react sensitively to a wider spectrum of events and peoples requires an overcoming of such cultural parochialism. But, in fact, few attain this broader vision. Some, of course, have little opportunity for wider cultural experience, though this condition should change as the movement of people accelerates. Others do not try to widen their experience because they prefer the old and familiar, seek from their affairs only further confirmation of the correctness of their own values. Still others recoil from such experiences because they feel it dangerous to probe too deeply into the personal or cultural unconscious. Exposure may reveal how tenuous and arbitrary many cultural norms are; such exposure might force people to acquire new bases for interpreting events. And even for the many who do seek actively to enlarge the variety of human beings with whom they are capable of communicating there are still difficulties.

Cultural myopia persists not merely because of inertia and habit, but chiefly because it is so difficult to overcome. One acquires a personality and a culture in childhood, long before he is capable of comprehending either of them. To survive, each person masters the perceptual orientations, cognitive biases, and communicative habits of his own culture. But once mastered, objective assessment of these same processes is awkward since the same mechanisms that are being evaluated must be used in making the evaluations. Once a child learns Japanese or English or Navaho, the categories and grammar of each language predispose him to perceive and think in certain ways, and discourage him from doing so in other ways. When he attempts to discover why he sees or thinks as he does, he uses the same techniques he is trying to identify. Once one becomes an Indian, an Ibo, or a Frenchman—or even a priest or scientist—it is difficult to extricate oneself from that mooring long enough to find out what one truly is or wants.

Fortunately, there may be a way around this paradox. Or promise of a way around it. It is to expose the culturally distinctive ways various peoples construe events and seek to identify the conventions that connect what is seen with what is thought with what is said. Once this cultural grammar is assimilated and the rules that govern the exchange of meanings are known, they can be shared and learned by those who choose to work and live in alien cultures.

When people within a culture face an insurmountable problem

they turn to friends, neighbors, associates, for help. To them they explain their predicament, often in distinctive personal ways. Through talking it out, however, there often emerge new ways of looking at the problem, fresh incentive to attack it, and alternative solutions to it. This sort of interpersonal exploration is often successful within a culture for people share at least the same communicative style even if they do not agree completely in their perceptions or beliefs.

When people communicate between cultures, where communicative rules as well as the substance of experience differs, the problems multiply. But so, too, do the number of interpretations and alternatives. If it is true that the more people differ the harder it is for them to understand each other, it is equally true that the more they differ the more they have to teach and learn from each other. To do so, of course, there must be mutual respect and sufficient curiosity to overcome the frustrations that occur as they flounder from one misunderstanding to another. Yet the task of coming to grips with differences in communicative styles—between or within cultures—is prerequisite to all other types of mutuality.

This book, then, attempts to explore and compare two cultures, particularly with regard to their communicative styles. It seeks to identify broad differences in the interpersonal orientations of Japanese and Americans. It attempts to describe, as specifically as possible, the ways in which they conduct their social encounters, and tries to expose the dynamic principles that govern them. Hopefully it may contribute in two distinct ways: First by helping people to better understand their own behavior; Second by contributing to the reduction of misunderstandings that spring not from destructive motives or contradictory beliefs, but from differences in manner and meaning. Without a serious and sustained effort to widen our universe of discourse no global village can possibly survive.

2 | Public and Private Self

It takes little sophistication to distinguish between the paintings of Utamaro and Picasso, the sculptures of Giacometti and Noguchi, the music of Beethoven and Brubeck, the novels of Kawabata and Dostoevsky. Even within a narrower range it requires only slightly more familiarity to recognize differences between the works of Mozart and Bach, Hiroshige and Hokusai, Kobo Abe and Yukio Mishima, the Beatles and the Rolling Stones.

Ordinary men, too, have a style of their own, a singular and consistent way of expressing themselves. Each person has a distinctive gait, mode of dress, way of gesturing; each shows some consistency in the frequency with which he speaks, his choice of words, the way he develops an argument or offers an apology. As the modern painter, Georges Braque, once noted, "One's style—it is in a way one's inability to do otherwise."[1]

Shortly after birth an infant learns to differentiate by touch and sound the presence of his mother or father, brother or sister. Within a year or two, he can imitate them. Before long he can do even better: he can cast them as actors in imaginary situations and, taking their roles, portray the way they would act and what they would say. In many cases he can construct lengthy dialogues that are devastatingly funny but embarrassingly true to life. The child is no longer merely repeating actions he has witnessed, but has grasped the inner dynamics of the personalities around him. Knowledge of the premises and strategies that govern the behavior of others makes prediction possible. This, in turn, contributes to successful communication with other people. Unfortunately, this sort of understanding is intuitive, it is known but cannot be articulated. As in riding a bicycle, a person knows, but cannot explain what it is that is known.

Cultures, too, have distinctive styles. They carry out their affairs according to different scripts. The presumption behind any investigation of cultural differences is simply this: that people nurtured in a common culture create and manifest their own unique personal styles out of a framework of assumptions and a system of symbols shared by members of that culture. Their habits of expression reveal sufficient uniformity that outsiders readily recognize the way Italians, Mexicans, or Koreans act and interact.

Every Japanese and every American "knows" the rules of his own culture in the sense of recognizing to whom and how he should communicate on a variety of occasions. But he knows in a private and unconscious way. He simply does what must be done or can be done in various interpersonal settings. And he relies unconsciously upon the grammar and techniques acquired in previous encounters. But, like any child, he seldom examines or is capable of examining objectively, the repertoire of message forms and rules from which he fashions his own personal style.

Anyone who has observed groups of Japanese or Americans talking together is aware at once of certain peculiarities in their habits of speech. In one group everyone bows and exchanges personal cards. When they speak they do so quietly, often in the form of understatements. Rarely does one hear a belligerent or unequivocal "No." Remarks are tailored to subtle differences in rank and relationship. Apologies come easily and often. People keep their distance, talk with their hands at their sides, seldom laugh or do so modestly.

In the other group they all shake hands as they begin a conversation. "No" is heard at least as often or more often than "Yes." There is impatience with any insistence upon status distinctions, within minutes they are referring to each other by first names. Conversational partners frequently touch each other to reinforce their statements, laugh often and loudly, and use their hands to punctuate nearly every remark. Arguments are heated, issues often polarized.

Which of these are superficial eccentricities and which are clues to critical differences in cultural perspectives? Which contribute to intercultural misunderstandings? What other similarities or contrasts in manner might be found? It was once said of the archaeologist Nelson Glueck that he could find "civilization in a shard." From a few fragments of clay pots he could reconstruct the institutions, the level of technology and the manner of daily life of an extinct culture. Can we, surrounded by the chatter of a thousand voices of living cultures similarly unravel some of the mysteries manifest in the different communicative styles of Japanese and Americans?

It can be persuasively argued that every object and every act of any culture has some meaning, from the design of an ashtray to the arranging of a marriage. That may be true, but some acts appear so accidental and so trivial that they reveal little, while others are so common and so crucial to the successful conduct of interpersonal encounters that they disclose much more. What is needed is some device to provide direction through the profusion of messages exchanged in any culture and to make comprehensible the seemingly random and contradictory features of everyday communicative acts.

The Use and Abuse of Models

In his book, *Resolving Social Conflicts*, Kurt Lewin suggests that some problems in interpreting human behavior might be simplified if scientists first developed theoretical models and then searched for facts to confirm or disprove them. The construction of such models has been widely followed by the physical scientists for centuries, and in recent decades has started to intrigue behavioral scientists as well. It seems to afford some way of dealing with unusually complex and often incomprehensible communicative acts.

Models may assume a variety of forms. Some are made of plastic, some of wood, some of switches and relays, some of toothpicks. They are often deceptively simple. Every child plays with or constructs them daily. His cars, airplanes, railroads and derricks are models in the sense that they replicate more or less accurately the appearance of their counterparts in reality. Models that reproduce or represent the form of some object are called structural models. The blueprints of architects, the drawings of geologists, the maps of oceanographers are of this type.

Students of human behavior require models that will reproduce processes, that will show how things operate rather than what they look like. It is not the appearance of the brain that presents problems for them, but how it functions. What they seek are prototypes that will explain fluctuations in attention, processes of decision-making, or the emergence of meanings. Even the often maligned common man employs rudimentary models to predict the reactions of his child or his tennis partner to comments he may make or actions he contemplates. But his constructs—the pictures in his head of the world outside—are rarely conscious, usually vague, and seldom tested in any systematic way. Yet they resemble in principle the theoretical models that scientists seek in their research.

These models accomplish in a concise way a number of valuable things: they clarify the theoretical position of the investigator; they identify critical variables; they permit a series of predictions to be made; and they are of great value in making his findings intelligible. Random and disconnected facts, no matter how numerous, are sometimes of less value than no facts at all. Like the pieces of a puzzle, or the clues to a mystery, the facts of life—or of communicative behavior—acquire value only as they can be put into meaningful relationships with each other. The use of models, then, can serve to identify the diverse motives and multiplicity of messages that peoples of different cultures use to conduct their affairs. And in so doing reveal the underlying dynamics that guide interaction within a social system.

Dimensions of the Self

Cultures, of course, do not communicate. Only individuals communicate. But cultures, through the patterns of personality they respect or punish, do influence the communicative manner of every member of society. Occasionally as a result of specific instructions, but more often by simply observing the actions of others, the individual learns what to notice or disregard, what is vital or trivial to survival, what should be censored or expressed, and to whom and in what form to express ideas and feelings. Cultures not only prefer certain kinds of information over others, but prefer certain modes of interpretation and expression. They value, in short, specific ways of encoding and decoding experience.

If one wants to identify the motives that prompt people to communicate, or seeks to account for the distinctive forms of messages in different cultures, the search must begin within the inner structure of the personality. For it is this inner assumptive world that mediates all meanings. One way of picturing this inner world is by means of the Johari Window.[2] It is a simple diagrammatic device for showing how meanings are processed within the organism, how problems of encoding and decoding are resolved. This intrapersonal process is, of course, the source of all interpersonal and intercultural acts. The basic dimensions of this diagram can be seen in the accompanying figure.

Figure 1   The Johari Window

	Known to Self	Unknown to Self
Known to Others	I Open (Shared)	II Blind (Repressed)
Unknown to Others	III Hidden (Denied)	IV Unknown

The first quadrant defines an area of shared information about the self. It includes all the things a person knows of himself that are known also to his associates and friends; it may include a wide variety of opinions and feelings that have been shared with others, or it may be limited to his address, phone number, position, occupation.

The second quadrant represents those aspects of the person of which he himself is ignorant. They may include motives or feelings that he rejects or denies, but are apparent to those who work or live with him. These might involve feelings of inadequacy, of optimism or pessimism, of strength or weakness, of desire for protection or independence.

Quadrant three constitutes knowledge of the self which the person, through careful monitoring and censoring of his words and acts, has kept from others. It may be that the person wishes to cover up or deny to others information about some past tragedy, some indiscretion, a personal weakness, a physical handicap, or even some private satisfaction. To some extent everyone presents and cultivates some kind of public image through control of what others are able to know about him.

Within the fourth quadrant is knowledge that is buried so deeply or so effectively camouflaged that neither the person nor his associates are aware of its existence. At least some aspects of the self remain inaccessible to every person, beyond his capacity to recognize or comprehend. Knowledge about ourselves, no matter how exhaustive, is never complete.

One personality might require a diagram that showed considerable repression over what others know; another personality might require one that expanded the area of information denied to the self. Changes in a personality, as a result of a close friendship or professional therapy, might also be indicated in "before" and "after" diagrams of personality structure.

The Johari Window does not automatically yield hypotheses that can be applied to interpersonal or intercultural behavior. But its major dimensions, "known to self" and "known to others," can be transformed into variables—the "public self" and "private self"—which might assist in exploring cultural differences. It was these variables that appeared promising in preliminary studies of the communicative behavior of Japanese and Americans. A careful examination of structural differences in personality appeared to offer some promise in clarifying and explaining the contrasting manner of interaction in the two cultures.

Public and Private Self in Japan

This investigation of communicative styles began with the postulation of a critical difference between Japanese and Americans with regard to the extent to which the self was exposed in everyday encounters. It was hypothesized that Japanese prefer an interpersonal style in which aspects of the self made accessible to others, the "public self," is relatively small, while the proportion that is not revealed, the "private self," is relatively large. Inner impulses, feelings, and attitudes are less readily shared with associates. If minimal exposure is the underlying unconscious motive in interpersonal relationships, this should manifest itself in a number of quite concrete ways: in the number and character of friendships, in topical preferences in conversation, in patterns of nonverbal interaction, even in customary responses to threat.

This hypothesis is expressed diagrammatically in the model shown in Figure 2. As later phases of the study are reported, it will be elaborated and refined. The "U" which lies at the center of the personality stands for the nearly inaccessible psychic assumptions and drives that comprise the unconscious. No person understands fully the sources of his words or actions. Surrounded by nearly impenetrable walls, this area of the self is rarely exposed to communication except in the most intimate human relationships or under professional treatment. Even then, unconscious impulses are seldom expressed directly but usually indirectly through the medium of dream, metaphor and fantasy.

The next area, identified as the "Private Self," marks off aspects of the person that are potentially communicable, but are not often or not usually shared with others. It consists of somewhat different material for every person—past experiences, feelings about the self and others, latent fears or personal needs—that they "know" or "can know" if they choose. But this sort of knowledge is not ordinarily shared unless the need is great or confidence in the other person is high. Then they may become the focus of conversation.

The outer area, the "Public Self," identifies aspects of the person that are readily available and easily shared with others. Again, the content of the public self differs for each person. It may consist of facts about one's work, personal tastes, family activities, opinions on public issues, or reactions to a multitude of daily events. Aside from small talk it comprises the commonest resource for carrying on conversation; information of this type is often volunteered or is willingly supplied in response to questions from others.

The extent of personal exposure when two Japanese converse is suggested in Figure 3. Generally only their public selves are engaged or exposed. The plus and minus signs that appear within this area of contact merely indicate that encounters within a culture can and do produce agreements and disagreements. But within the boundaries of a shared communicative style—among people who occupy the same universe of discourse—the meaning of a gesture or a word or a silence is likely to provoke a similar reaction even if the conclusion to which the message points does not. In this sense, members of the same culture may disagree, but they are less likely to misunderstand. When disagreements occur, as they do in all cultures, the conflict is readily recognized and can often be resolved in some way.

If this postulate regarding the relatively larger area of the private as compared to the public self among Japanese is correct, what specific effects might be manifest in their communicative behavior? It is hypothesized that, in comparison with Americans, the follow-

Figure 2 Japanese Public and Private Self

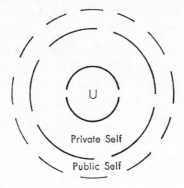

Figure 3 Japanese Interpersonal Communication

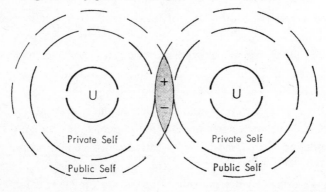

ing predictions will hold in interpersonal encounters between Japanese:

1. THE JAPANESE SHOULD INTERACT MORE SELECTIVELY AND WITH FEWER PERSONS. Communication is safer with acquaintances and intimate friends since they know and will respect private limits on self revelation. The risk of exceeding such norms is multiplied in encounters with strangers whose communicative styles may be unpredictable.

2. THE JAPANESE SHOULD PREFER REGULATED TO SPONTANEOUS FORMS OF COMMUNICATION. Conventional communicative forms, because they carry a lower risk of accidental exposure of the private self, should constitute a higher proportion of social experience. Rituals and pastimes, where conversation follows prescribed patterns, should be preferred to more spontaneous forms such as personal encounters and intimacy. The greater the formality surrounding interpersonal meetings the smaller the chance of exceeding conventional limits on personal revelation.

3. THE JAPANESE, ACROSS A VARIETY OF TOPICS, SHOULD COMMUNICATE LESS OF THEMSELVES VERBALLY AND PREFER A LOWER DEGREE OF PERSONAL INVOLVEMENT. Not only will more formal encounters be preferred to more informal ones, but the content of conversation itself will tend to be less revealing of the self. External events will be seen as more appropriate topics of discussion than inner reactions. Across all topics it is expected there will be less disclosure of private opinion and personal feeling.

4. THE JAPANESE WILL TEND TO LIMIT PHYSICAL AS WELL AS VERBAL EXPRESSIVENESS. Since physical acts, as well as words, are indicators of inner emotional states, it may be expected that physical contact and physical expression may be reduced. Limiting the number of channels through which inner states may be transmitted reduces the possibility that aspects of the self that are private may be disclosed.

5. THE JAPANESE WILL PREFER TO COPE WITH THREATENING INTERPERSONAL SITUATIONS BY ADOPTING PREDOMINANTLY PASSIVE RATHER THAN ACTIVE FORMS OF DEFENSE. The more of the self that is guarded, the more one is vulnerable in social encounters; thus there is greater need to remain alert to potentially embarrassing situations. Furthermore, since defensive modes tend to be consistent with prevailing interpersonal orientations, the Japanese should react so as to reduce the intensity of personal

involvement and to limit further expression of private meanings.

6. THE JAPANESE, SINCE THEY EXPOSE AND EXPLORE INNER REACTIONS LESS OFTEN AND LESS THOROUGHLY, MAY BE LESS WELL KNOWN TO THEMSELVES. Limited communication of the self is likely to restrict the occasions and lower the intensity of interpersonal conflict. But if disclosure to others is a major means of exposure to the self, Japanese may show less insight into self and have less accurate perceptions of self.

Public and Private Self in America

The same variables, the public self and the private self, can be used to describe the distinguishing features of American interpersonal behavior. (See Figures 4 and 5.) It is postulated that Americans, in general, prefer a communicative style in which the self made accessible to others is relatively larger, the proportion that remains concealed is relatively smaller. This suggests that what an American knows about himself—his opinions, attitudes, impulses, feelings—is more readily shared with others. This principle of maximum personal exposure should manifest itself in his range of friendships, preferred types of communicative encounters, topical interests, and typical responses to threat.

If this hypothesis is correct, what specific behaviors should be evident when Americans interact? It is suggested that, in comparison with the Japanese, the following predictions should characterize interpersonal encounters among Americans:

1. THE AMERICANS SHOULD COMMUNICATE WITH A LARGER NUMBER OF PERSONS AND LESS SELECTIVELY. They may be less discriminating in whom they talk with, even choosing unpredictable strangers on occasion, since there is less to censor. They may also be more consistent in communicative manner with a broader

Figure 4   American Public and Private Self

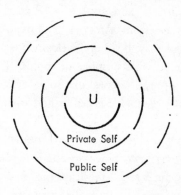

Figure 5   American Interpersonal Communication

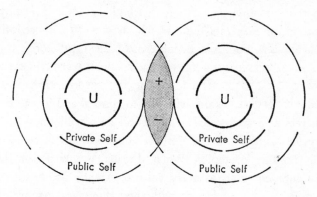

range of conversational partners.

2. THE AMERICANS SHOULD PREFER MORE SPONTANEOUS FORMS
OF COMMUNICATION TO MORE RITUALIZED ONES. Formal encounters,
where conversation conforms to restrictive norms and rules, should
occupy a smaller proportion of their social experience, because they
interfere with fuller expression of the self. Ritualized interactions
may be less attractive to them.

3. THE AMERICANS SHOULD COMMUNICATE THEIR VIEWS MORE

FULLY AND ON A MORE PERSONAL LEVEL ACROSS A VARIETY OF TOPICS. Polite phrases and superficial exchanges may provoke impatient reactions from Americans. Private disclosures and personal opinions may be more welcomed as contributions to conversation over a wide number of topics. There may be less concern with the appropriateness of a subject for conversation, and the boundaries between what is public and what is private may be less rigid.

4. THE AMERICANS WILL TEND TO CULTIVATE PHYSICAL AS WELL AS VERBAL INTIMACY. Since the aim is to seek more complete expression of the inner self, Americans may not only disclose more fully verbally, but may try to utilize as many channels of communication as possible. For this reason they may display greater physical animation and engage in a higher frequency of physical contact during conversation. Touch, as one of the more intimate forms of interaction, may be more encouraged and more accepted.

5. THE AMERICANS WILL PREFER TO COPE WITH THREATENING INTERPERSONAL ENCOUNTERS BY ADOPTING PREDOMINANTLY ACTIVE FORMS OF DEFENSE. Again, with less to conceal and less to censor, vulnerability is reduced. There should be a willingness to communicate with a wider variety of conversational partners on a wider number of topics. When threatened interpersonally, an experience common to every culture, Americans should prefer defenses that are consistent with their dominant manner. They should, thus, favor more active responses since they permit deeper involvement and provide still further opportunity for self expression.

6. THE AMERICANS, SINCE THEY EXPOSE THEIR INNER REACTIONS MORE FREQUENTLY AND FULLY, SHOULD BE BETTER KNOWN TO THEMSELVES. More complete communication of the self should increase the frequency and deepen the intensity of interpersonal conflict. Still, fuller knowledge of the self should follow from fuller

expression of the self. If this is true then Americans may display somewhat greater self insight and reveal more accurate perceptions of themselves.

What is postulated, therefore, is a difference not of kind, but of degree, between the psychic structure of Japanese and Americans. But a difference that is significant rather than trivial. This contrast in personality structure, reflecting cultural assumptions and values, should cause members of the two societies to talk differently, about different topics, in different ways, to different people, with different consequences.

An Intercultural Communication Model

Before proceeding to test the hypothesis above it may be useful to examine a model of intercultural communication, and to speculate on sources of confusion or tension that might arise from encounters between Japanese and Americans. If such differences exist in communicative styles within these cultures, what might occur when members of the two cultures meet? The consequences, of course, will become clearer as the data unfold, but they may be anticipated in a theoretical sense here.

The models, Figures 6 and 7, portray hypothetical conversations between a Japanese and an American. As these diagrams suggest, there are not only the normal areas of agreement and disagreement that can be expected to arise in any discussion (shown by the + and − signs in the lightly shaded area), but these are now compounded and aggravated by differences in communicative intent and style (the − signs appearing in the darker area). Each person seeks to fashion the relationship according to his own rhetorical tradition; each strives to impose a different definition of the situation, a different degree of personal involvement, a different form

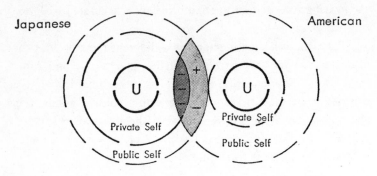

Figure 6 Intercultural Communication: American Style

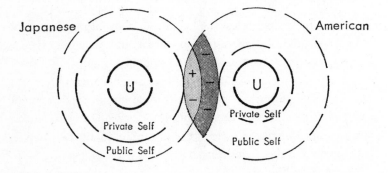

Figure 7 Intercultural Communication: Japanese Style

and pace for the conversation; each tries to suggest an agenda, a pattern of discussion, and a set of procedures appropriate in his own culture.

In the first instance the American conversational norms prevail, either because of their forceful assertion by the American or the reluctance of the Japanese to resist them. In the second instance the Japanese conversational norms prevail, again because of the insistence of the Japanese or the unwillingness of the American to oppose them. In most cases some tenous compromise or vacillation between the two conversational modes will result. But neither of these outcomes will eliminate feelings of awkwardness and frustration.

As each—blindly conforming to his own cultural script—asserts his own approach to problems, his own level of frankness, his own evaluations of the situation, each finds he lacks a frame for comprehending the other. One may be frightened at the prospect of being communicatively invaded; the other is annoyed at the prospect of endless formalities. The very cues that were impeccable guides to meanings within their cultures have turned into obstacles to the comprehension of messages from the other's culture.

The Japanese may be frustrated in his contacts with Americans by their "flippant" attitude toward formalities, their "insensitivity" to differences in status, their "embarrassing" critical remarks, their "prying" questions, their "unnatural" physical intimacy, their predilection for "premature" decisions. In the Japanese culture these are the meanings that would be attached to such behavior. How is one to know, or if he knows, to overcome his natural inclination to follow the only rules one knows for making sense—his own?

The American talking to a Japanese associate is similarly baffled by rituals that seem "endless," conversations that seem "pointless," by long silences that "waste time," by humor that seems "childish," by delays that are "inexcusable," by "evasive" statements, by the "distant and cold" demeanor of his counterpart. Like his foreign associate, how is he to know, or if he knows, to overcome his inclination to interpret behavior according to the rules of his own culture? What seems clear to one is patently unclear to the other. And what seems to be clear may actually be misunderstood!

The Japanese, with the best of motives, wants to show kindness or respect to the visiting American. So he showers him with attention, plans his itinerary, escorts him to every attraction, supervises each photograph, selects a menu for him, chooses his souvenirs, and honors him with farewell gifts. The intent is constructive, but the American may interpret this as "coercive hospitality" at best, or at worst as "damned interference." He may appreciate the motive, but prefers to select his own itinerary, move at his own pace, choose his own restaurant, and spontaneously change plans according to his mood at the moment. After exhaustion has taken over he may feel more anger than gratitude for the "hospitality" he received.

Or the American, again with the best of intentions, wants to convey his appreciation for some great kindness shown him by his Japanese colleague. So, as in the United States, he compliments him warmly and effusively for his thoughtfulness. But in Japan gratitude is only occasionally expressed directly between work associates and rarely between members of a family or close friends. Compliments are ritualized exchanges between people who do not know each other well. When people are close friends gratitude is gratuitous; it is assumed each will be thoughtful of the other. So the compliment that is spoken may be heard as an evidence of distance rather than as an indicator of affection.

Every culture maintains some boundary between meaning and nonsense. It does so by distinguishing between signals—cues to which the culture assigns specific meaning—and noises—cues which the culture ignores or sees as devoid of meaning. The dividing line is invisible, symbolic rather than real. But it is no less significant for this reason: the success of every human interaction hinges on it.

The Asian fails to tip the taxi driver, the waitress or the bellhop. Not because he intends any insult, but because he is unaware of any payment being required. After all, he has just paid for their services. The Westerner fails to attach any significance to walking on *tatami* in his street shoes. It is, after all, only another style of carpeting. What is noise in one culture is often signal in another; what is signal in one is only noise in the other.

When agreements concerning the boundary which separates signals and noise break down, as they do when people of different cultures communicate, useful symbols dissolve into gibberish. Lacking any way of calibrating the two codes, of establishing some correspondence between them, the members of contrasting cultures may suspend all efforts to reach each other. Every attempt only seems to drive them farther apart. In their confusion they often surrender to indifference or to hostility.

The Exploration of Cultural Differences

In a sense this is both the worst and the best of times in which to study communication between cultures: it is the worst of times for never have cultures displayed so much volatility, been so fragmented internally, or been so subject to alien influences; it is the best of times for never has access to foreign cultures been so easy, cultural artifacts—books, films, newspapers, objects—so available for analysis, or the necessity of enlarging intercultural understanding so crucial to our mutual survival.

Yet there are unavoidable risks in the investigation of any subject as broad and complex as intercultural communication. One of these is the perpetual danger of divorce between description and explanation, between fact and theory. Anyone who has ever travelled abroad can appreciate how easy it is to find reinforcement of existing stereotypes wherever one looks, or how tempting it is to frame explanations of an alien culture out of single happy or unhappy experience. If staring too long at the stars contributes to tripping over the realities of life, so may focusing too exclusively on the ground contribute to losing one's way. Having formulated our theoretical bearings, it is imperative to examine the actual form and conduct of interpersonal affairs in these two cultures.

A number of instruments were used to gather data on the communicative styles of Japanese and Americans. The chapters that follow report findings obtained from a Role Description Checklist, a Self Disclosure Scale, a Nonverbal Inventory, and a Defensive Strategy Scale. They reveal to whom Japanese and Americans talk, what they talk about, how much they disclose of themselves, what kind of nonverbal contact they maintain, and how they defend themselves against threatening remarks.

The studies, initiated in 1968, were completed in 1972. The subjects questioned about their communicative behavior were Japanese and American college students between the ages of 18 and 24. All but one of the samples consisted of two hundred and forty subjects divided equally between the two cultures and composed of equal numbers of males and females. A college sample, of course, is not representative of the entire population of either country. But no limited sample would be. And this age group offers certain advantages. First, the young are an important segment of society and may be more sensitive to its values than their parents. Second, if the shape of the future is to be found, it must be sought among those who will create it. Finally, and most important, if there is increased exchange between East and West, especially among the younger generation, any data secured from them will minimize rather than magnify any cultural differences that may be found. Thus any conclusions drawn from the findings should reflect a conservative rather than a radical bias.

It is difficult to dissect any culture and expose its underlying premises. The accurate description of everyday conversation is itself complicated enough. But one hopes to do better than that, to find reliable relationships among these behaviors, and to interpret their significance. Perhaps the best, if not the only, way of doing this is to compare one culture with another.

Every cross-cultural study does this implicitly for the investigator cannot help but view the foreign culture from the vantage of his own. For this reason it might be better to make any comparisons as explicit and visible as possible so readers themselves can test the conclusions and propose alternative interpretations of their own. Here the focus is upon the communicative style of the Japanese using the communicative behavior of Americans as a comparative base. Hopefully it will be followed by many other cultural comparisons, particularly one that examines American communicative style from the perspective of Japanese interaction.

One final qualification. The reader may wonder how any outsider can discover anything important about the inner rationale of a culture that is "foreign" to him. Should such research not be put in the hands of people already familiar with the culture and able to operate with daily effectiveness in it? The answer is that it is the familiarity of the native-born that often places him at a disadvantage. It is no accident that the most penetrating books on America are by Alexis De Tocqueville who was French and Geoffrey Gorer who is English. Among the most provocative on Japan, too, are those of Ronald Dore who is English, Ruth Benedict who is American, and Fosco Maraini who is Italian. Naïvete has a double edge. It permits one to question acts that are so automatic and unconscious that members of a culture rarely notice them. Yet it may also predispose one to misinterpret because his own cultural biases intrude upon the significance he attaches to these acts. Innocence, then, gives rise to questions about a culture, but only systematic investigation provides the means of finding the answers and testing their accuracy.

3 | Profiles of Two Cultures

Assume you have been asked to observe from a distance two groups of people involved in social interaction. Could one recognize, from physical appearance alone, which were Japanese and which were Americans? Probably. One group would include predominantly people with black hair, brown eyes, round faces, small noses, and shorter bodies. The other would manifest a wider variety of hair and eye color, longer faces, larger noses, and taller bodies.

Now assume that it is impossible to distinguish between the groups on the basis of physical features, but they can only be identified on the basis of their conversational manner. Members of the two groups can be studied as they enter a room, introduce each other, take their seats, select a leader, engage in discussion, explore differences of opinion, and conclude their conversation. Without relying upon differences in language, could one still ascertain which group was composed of Japanese and which of Americans? Probably. Although with some groups physical attributes may be better clues to cultural identity, with others social attributes may be as reliable, and in some cases more reliable, indicators.

Any effort to compare cultural patterns of communicative behavior might reasonably begin with an effort to identify the dominant features of interaction within each society. What are the general characteristics of Japanese and American communicative behavior? In what respects are members of these two cultures alike in interpersonal encounters? In what respects do they differ? And are these differences serious enough to warrant taking a closer look at the precise form and content of specific messages? There is little reason to undertake a laborious microscopic dissection of habits of talk unless there are grounds for suspecting that critical differences in communicative style exist.

Earlier it was postulated that Japanese and Americans may differ with regard to accessibility of the self in communication. It was predicted that Japanese prefer more regulated encounters, interact more guardedly, disclose relatively less of themselves, and tend to withdraw when threatened. Americans, it was suggested, prefer less regulated encounters, are more self assertive, become more involved and respond more actively to threats from others. Do they see themselves and see each other in ways that support these speculations?

Role Description Checklist

What is sought is a broad profile of the communicative styles of Japanese and Americans. To identify these collective features a "Role Description Checklist" was adapted from one used to study differences in individual patterns of communication. It provides a set of thirty adjectives to describe the attributes a person displays in relations with significant other people. Each person completes the form by selecting the five adjectives that best describe his manner of interacting with his Mother, Father, Same Sex Friend, Opposite Sex Friend, Superior, Subordinate, Child and Disliked Person. From it one can derive a measure of the degree of consistency in interpersonal behavior. Over a period of years the list has been tested to eliminate words people rarely use in self descriptions and to add terms that people felt were needed to account for their behavior. The thirty adjectives making up the final list have proven valuable in identifying differences in personal styles. Within the American culture there has been no need to add further terms, and nearly every adjective is chosen by some respondent at each administration of the test.

The Role Description Checklist, useful as it might be in defining personal styles within a culture, should also be useful in differentiating between societies since they represent a synthesis of personal styles. The concept of a "generalized personality" is often employed in making cultural comparisons. A pilot study in Japan reinforced confidence in this instrument, but indicated the need for some revision. Precise equivalents had to be found for all thirty adjectives, and some new terms were clearly needed so the list would include qualities cultivated specifically by the Japanese society and commonly used by Japanese in describing each other.

A committee of bilingual faculty, staff and students, drawn from the Language Division of International Christian University, was formed to accomplish this. Japanese equivalents were agreed upon and four new terms added: *Amaeru*—To Seek a Protective Relationship;[1] *Jikoshucho o suru*—Self Assertive; *Enryo o suru*—Reserved; and *Kudaketa*—Spontaneous. The final list consisted of the thirty original adjectives and the four new terms.

The instructions were simple: Subjects were asked to read the entire list of adjectives and then to select the five words that "best describe what Americans are like in talking to each other" and "best describe what Japanese are like in talking to each other." A total of one hundred and twenty-two Japanese college students and a total of forty-two American college students enrolled in classes in Japan completed this form. Practical difficulties made it impossible to obtain a larger sample of Americans with sufficient exposure to both cultures. But both sets of subjects had regular contact with members of the opposite culture, and hence had opportunity to observe them and form private judgments. Due to college requirements, both Japanese and American subjects were able to speak both languages or were enrolled in intensive courses of language instruction.

Japanese Profile

The frequency with which each of the terms was selected as descriptive of the communicative characteristics of Japanese is indicated in Figure 8. By drawing a line connecting the scores on each adjective a silhouette or profile of their communicative manner may be obtained. When this is done the dominant features of Japanese communicative style stand out in sharp relief: that is, there is a substantial gap separating adjectives that are frequently and seldom chosen.

The Japanese see themselves as "Reserved," "Formal," "Silent," "Cautious," "Evasive," and "Serious" in that order. All these terms were chosen by nearly half or more of the respondents. Even the two next most chosen adjectives—"Distant" and "Dependent"—seem consistent with the configuration suggested by the most chosen terms. Since "To seek a protective relationship" resembles or overlaps "Dependent," it might also be counted among their cultural attributes.

The characteristics of Japanese communicative style as seen

Figure 8　Japanese Cultural Profiles

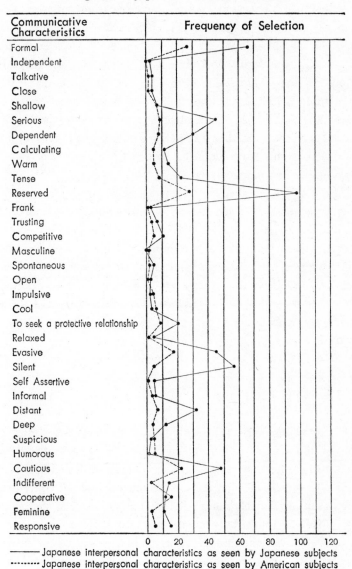

Communicative Characteristics	Frequency of Selection

Formal
Independent
Talkative
Close
Shallow
Serious
Dependent
Calculating
Warm
Tense
Reserved
Frank
Trusting
Competitive
Masculine
Spontaneous
Open
Impulsive
Cool
To seek a protective relationship
Relaxed
Evasive
Silent
Self Assertive
Informal
Distant
Deep
Suspicious
Humorous
Cautious
Indifferent
Cooperative
Feminine
Responsive

0　20　40　60　80　100　120

———— Japanese interpersonal characteristics as seen by Japanese subjects
·········· Japanese interpersonal characteristics as seen by American subjects

through American eyes also appear in Figure 8. Despite differences in magnitude due to variations in sample size, there appears to be nearly complete agreement in the relative ordering of the terms. These respondents, too, describe the Japanese as "Reserved," "Formal," "Cautious," and "Evasive." There are only two differences in the profiles: Americans place "Silent" lower on the list of attributes, and place "Cooperative" higher than do the Japanese. "Serious" and "Dependent" move to somewhat lower positions on the scale, the latter perhaps reflecting a lower cultural sensitivity to this attribute. But the overall picture obtained from both sets of respondents is substantially the same.

The features ascribed to be characteristic of communication among Japanese, it would appear, conform closely to predictions derived from the original models. On the whole Japanese people seem to prefer more formal and more regulated encounters, tend to be reserved and cautious in expressing themselves, prefer to be evasive and silent rather than open and frank. The picture one obtains is of a rather highly contained self which is controlled and cautiously expressed and a larger private self that is hidden or unknown.

American Profile

To obtain a picture of the communicative style of Americans we can, as above, record the frequency with which each attribute is chosen and plot these points so they provide a profile of American characteristics. As before, the interpersonal manner of Americans stands out in relatively sharp relief, though not quite as sharply as the Japanese profile. This might be expected, since the Japanese culture is an extreme case of cultural homogeneity and the American culture an extreme case of cultural heterogeneity. Still, the

Figure 9 American Cultural Profile

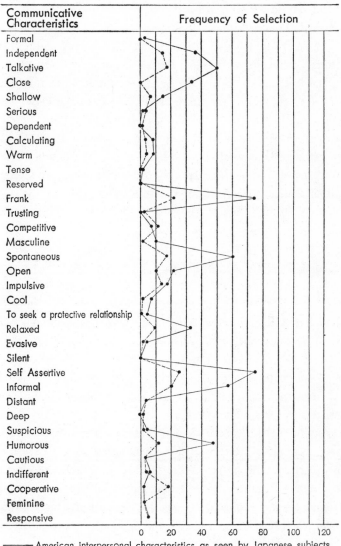

Communicative Characteristics / Frequency of Selection

Formal
Independent
Talkative
Close
Shallow
Serious
Dependent
Calculating
Warm
Tense
Reserved
Frank
Trusting
Competitive
Masculine
Spontaneous
Open
Impulsive
Cool
To seek a protective relationship
Relaxed
Evasive
Silent
Self Assertive
Informal
Distant
Deep
Suspicious
Humorous
Cautious
Indifferent
Cooperative
Feminine
Responsive

0   20   40   60   80   100   120

———— American interpersonal characteristics as seen by Japanese subjects
-------- American interpersonal characteristics as seen by American subjects

frequencies that divide the high and low choices are substantial and present no problem of interpretation.

Japanese respondents see Americans as "Self Assertive," "Frank," "Spontaneous," "Informal," "Talkative," and "Humorous." Following these most chosen attributes are "Independent," "Close," and "Relaxed." Again, the latter terms introduce no contradiction with the pattern obtained from the higher frequency adjectives.

American perceptions of themselves also appear in Figure 9. Despite differences in absolute frequencies that arise from discrepancies in sample sizes, there appears to be substantial, if not complete, agreement. Americans, too, describe themselves as "Self Assertive," "Frank," "Informal," "Spontaneous," and "Talkative." Thus, although there are slight differences in the ordering of these terms, there is surprising agreement in the overall picture. Again, the results appear to conform closely to the predictions made from the theoretical models. In general, Americans appear to be more "Self Assertive" and "Self Expressive," to seek more informal encounters with each other, to be more spontaneous and talkative, and to be more open and frank in revealing themselves. If the Japanese can be characterized as "contained," the Americans would appear to be more "expansive."

Perhaps the single best clue to the interpersonal orientations in these two cultures is found in the adjectives most frequently chosen to describe each cultural style and chosen by nearly every person in both samples: "Reserved" for Japanese and "Self Assertive" for Americans. In any case, the findings contribute support to the idea for Americans of a larger public self that is expressed more completely and candidly, and for Japanese of a more limited public self that is less completely and cautiously expressed.

Cultural Contrasts

One more perspective from which to explore these findings is obtained by pooling the data from both sets of respondents and constructing composite profiles of the two cultures. These profiles may then be placed on a single graph and studied to see in what respects the communicative styles differ from each other. Although it is immediately clear that the two cultures do differ in their interpersonal orientations, the exact nature of this difference is important. Do they each merely manifest different attributes, or do they occupy polar positions along the same dimensions?

When examined the data give a visual impression not only of difference but of contradiction. (See Figure 10.) Although some of the adjectives attributed to each culture might appear independent of the other, the vast majority of both chosen and rejected terms seem to lie along the same interpersonal dimensions. "Formal" and "Informal," "Silent" and "Talkative," "Reserved" and "Spontaneous," "Evasive" and "Frank" are not merely distinctive cultural characteristics, but constitute the polar extremes along a single set of attributes.

This impression is strengthened by noting the singular pattern of the scores. The qualities most frequently attributed to the Japanese are "Reserved," "Formal," "Cautious," "Evasive," "Silent," "Serious," and "Dependent." All score above forty on the Role Description Checklist which means that roughly one-fourth or more of all respondents chose these as typical of Japanese communication. American scores on these same attributes ranged between zero ("Reserved," "Silent") and five ("Serious") at the very highest.

The same conclusion draws support from an examination of

Figure 10 Composite Cultural Profile

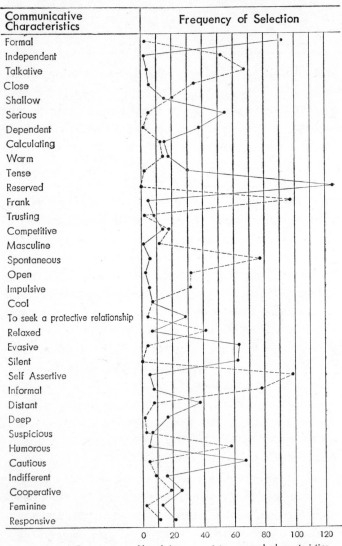

Communicative Characteristics / Frequency of Selection

Formal
Independent
Talkative
Close
Shallow
Serious
Dependent
Calculating
Warm
Tense
Reserved
Frank
Trusting
Competitive
Masculine
Spontaneous
Open
Impulsive
Cool
To seek a protective relationship
Relaxed
Evasive
Silent
Self Assertive
Informal
Distant
Deep
Suspicious
Humorous
Cautious
Indifferent
Cooperative
Feminine
Responsive

0   20   40   60   80   100   120

——— Composite profile of Japanese interpersonal characteristics
------- Composite profile of American interpersonal characteristics

the composite profile of Americans. The qualities most often attributed to them are "Self Assertive," "Frank," "Informal," "Spontaneous," "Talkative," "Humorous," "Independent," and "Relaxed." All these adjectives score above forty and were also chosen by at least one-fourth of all respondents. On only two of them, "Relaxed" and "Informal," do the Japanese score above five.

In short, the distance that divides these two cultures is so enormous along the same interpersonal dimensions that it is difficult to avoid concluding that they are nearly exact opposites. The qualities that one society nurtures—reserve, formality, and silence in one case, and self assertion, informality, and talkativeness in the other—are the same qualities the other society discourages. If this is true, then studies of communicative behavior within these two countries may be of singular value. And investigation of communication between them may be an especially promising place in which to expose and clarify the impact of such differences in communicative manner upon interpersonal and international relations.

Commentary: Japanese Profile

Other sources of information on Japanese cultural characteristics appear to confirm the profiles reported here. In an earlier study Japanese students were asked to formulate ten statements that best described their personal modes of interacting with others. Under the heading, "What I am Like in Interpersonal Relations," they commented along the following lines: "I try to behave according to my role and circumstance," "I try to be as polite as possible," "I pretend to be calm and cool, even when I am not," "I rarely show my true self," "I don't say all of what I think," "I try to keep the conversation happy and pleasant," "I use words that won't hurt anybody," "I try not to disagree," "I escape difficult questions," "I always smile when I talk," "I try to agree, even when I don't," "I try to behave smoothly," "I avoid saying anything that would hurt others," "I feel uneasy and tense in a group," "I never talk about inner feelings." These sentiments and descriptions repeated frequently in different words appear to be only elaborations of such terms as "reserved," "formal," "cautious," and "evasive."

A recent study by Midori Shigeta analyzed in depth the differences in Japanese and American ways of communicating an apology, a request, and a refusal.[2] She found that sensitivity to status differences was clearly manifest in the messages of Japanese while Americans showed more consciousness of the closeness of the personal relationship apart from any consideration of status. When it came to the form and content of the messages her analysis indicated that the Japanese manner was more indirect, more ambiguous, and less explicit and logical.

There has been, also, an uninterrupted stream of foreign observers who have tried to absorb and distill the subtle and complex character of Japanese life. Each has used his own vocabulary or coined his own metaphor to capture the Japanese ambience. But when these writers discuss social relationships among Japanese their remarks bear a striking affinity to the empirical data just reported. Donald Richie, in an article entitled "The Japanese Character," describes Japan as a "land of a time and a place for everything," where role-playing and role-living substitute for individuality of thought and action.[3]

In her now classic study, *The Chrysanthemum and the Sword*, Benedict found an analogy between Japanese personality and the lacquer for which the country is famous.[4] Both are slowly acquired, present a beautiful surface to the world, and are as much admired as the substance they cover. The Japanese, she found, arranged their lives to the last detail to avoid shame-arousing situations, feared ostracism and social disapproval more than self-repression or self-denial. Propriety, behavior that conforms to the norms regulating human intercourse, was far more important to them than honesty in self expression or the preservation of personal integrity.

Halloran, in *Japan: Images and Realities*, contrasts the subordination of the individual in the East with his deification in the West. In a chapter entitled "We the Japanese" he synthesizes the interpersonal attitudes of a typical but fictitious Japanese: "As I grew up, my parents taught me to keep my own thoughts to myself if I didn't agree with other people. It is very important, they said, that my actions and thoughts be in harmony with the actions and thoughts of other people with whom I have a personal relationship, and to subordinate myself to our family and the school and the company."[5] Robert Guillain, who has had a lifetime of involvement with Japan, comments on the Japanese "veil of remarkable politeness," the outward calm that masks a tension of which outsiders are unaware, and the preference of Japanese for "social contacts that are more pleasant than deep."[6]

Japan, of course, has suffered no lack of sensitive analysts of her own. Specialists with training in a variety of disciplines concur in noting an emphasis on decorum, propriety, and conformity. In his massive study entitled *Ways of Thinking of Eastern Peoples*, Hajime Nakamura emphasizes the overriding importance to the Japanese of membership in and preservation of a "limited social nexus."[7] This tight bond of limited social scope is preserved through social rituals, elaborate forms of personal address, sensitive observance of rules of conduct, suppression of criticism, and avoidance of candid remarks. Kiyoshi Seike, in describing the other-oriented character of Japanese behavior, puts it more succinctly: "He does what he is expected to do, he says what he is expected to say, he abides by an intricate code of etiquette."[8]

The noted anthropologist, Chie Nakane, after describing the vertical structure of Japanese society, notes the way this structure invades personal relationships and regulates conversation, preventing direct exchanges of divergent opinions in decision making: "One would prefer to be silent than utter such words as 'no' or 'I disagree.' The avoidance of such open and bald negative expressions is rooted in the fear that it might disrupt the harmony and order of the group."[9] The underlying dialectic in Japanese social relationships appears to favor preservation of a delicate rapport among the members of a collective rather than a confrontation between independent judgments as in the United States. Yoshiharu Matsumoto, too, contrasts the "collectivity orientations" that dominate Japanese social relations with the "self orientations" that dominate the American social scene.[10]

Studies undertaken by behavioral scientists have probed such cultural differences in depth. And, in general, they confirm the interpersonal attributes reported here. Mario Abate and F. Berrien, for example, in a study employing nearly a thousand subjects in Japan and the United States, found great consistency within each culture and great inconsistency between them. The Japanese, who scored high on deference, order, affiliation, and achievement contrasted with Americans who scored high on dominance, exhibition, autonomy, and change.[11]

The Thematic Apperception Test was used by William Caudill to reveal the personality structure of persons of Japanese ancestry in the United States. After subjects were shown a series of photographs they were asked to make up stories about them. The ambiguity of the pictures, however, required viewers to project their own biases onto the scenes, making it possible to identify cultural assumptions and orientations. His study, one of the most penetrating in methodology, showed the Japanese as manifesting deference to parents, concern with social acceptance, compliance with expectations of others, care in social conduct, and inhibition of aggressive impulses.[12]

Walter Fenz and Abe Arkoff in a contrastive study of Caucasian, Chinese, Filipino and Japanese students in Hawaii found the Japanese were "comparatively high on deference and lowest of any group on dominance, highest in the need for abasement and low in the need for aggression. They were also highest in their expression of the need for nurturance."[13]

Commentary: American Profile

The American cultural scene, like the Japanese, has not gone unnoticed or unremarked. Observers of many persuasions have poked about in American institutions and manners. Historically they stretch from Hector St. John de Crevecoeur to David Riesman. They come in many varieties, foreign and domestic: they include Denis Brogan, Luigi Barzini, S. N. Eisenstadt, Julian Marias among the "outsiders" and Max Lerner, Walter Lippman, Margaret Mead, and C. Wright Mills among the "insiders."

Unfortunately, the features of the American landscape that are most often noted are its political and sociological characteristics. Harold Laski's monumental work, *The American Democracy*, is illustrative of the former while Gunnar Myrdal's *The American Dilemma* is representative of the latter. Occasionally, buried in the exposition of other topics, there are reflections on the depth and quality of human interaction.

Several themes dominate these reflections.[14] Many writers emphasize the "informality" of Americans, their "ease with strangers," their "infectious exhibitionism," their "spontaneity," their "propensity for argument." The Israeli sociologist, S. N. Eisenstadt, sees them "formalizing informality," encouraging open and easy personal relationships, rewarding spontaneity, frankness and individual expression. Peter von Zahn, too, remarks that they are a "people without forms," without guides for the conduct of social intercourse, yet driven by this fact to create new ways of negotiating differences and working together.

An Indian writer, A. D. Gorwala, admits Americans are approachable, gregarious, unrestrained, and fond of conversation, but finds them also prone to "loud talk," "boasting," and "brash statements." Mochtar Lubis, an Indonesian, sees Americans as demonstrative and articulate, quick to show love or hate, impatient with forms and irreverent toward superiors, preferring straight answers to straight questions. In these respects they contrast sharply with the modest and polite habits of his own people. Though admittedly honest and direct, he finds Americans lacking in peace of mind, serenity, in capacity for inner contemplation. The American smile of greeting draws reactions from many: some feel it is indicative of warmth and openness; others find it an artificial and empty social gesture.

Consistent throughout nearly all observations is an emphasis upon the sacredness of the individual and upon its communicative consequences. Self expression rather than self containment appears the dominant social motive. To certain observers this emphasis upon noisy and blunt self assertion is invigorating and appealing, while others reject it in favor of a style that emphasizes sensitivity to social distinctions and respect for social harmony. "Life in America," says Morris Broughton, "is lived from outward within and not from within outward."[15]

Few of the social critics cited can match the breadth or depth of insights found in one of the earliest commentators on America, Alexis De Tocqueville, or one of the more recent, Geoffrey Gorer.

De Tocqueville traces the interpersonal style of Americans to their commitment to individualism, and to its deeper source in egalitarianism. "Equality," he writes, "begets in man the desire for judging everything for himself." This, in turn, diminishes respect for tradition, for social convention, for authority, for propriety. Nothing should restrict or delay the expression of every thought and impulse. And if this encourages conversation that is natural, spontaneous, unaffected and honest, it cultivates no less a tendency toward excessive verbalization, argumentativeness, rudeness and exaggeration. Americans may attach great importance to the substance of what is said, but may ignore the form of its expression.[16]

Gorer, too, feels that the rejection of authority and of external forms of discipline shape American patterns of speech. To him the people of the United States seem as pained by any deference to the status of others as the Japanese are shamed by social improprieties arising from indifference to such distinctions. From infancy to adulthood, Gorer argues, the American child is surrounded by an appreciative audience continuously encouraging self expression, but also cultivating exaggerated and continuous verbalization. "Modern America," he writes, "is perhaps more than any other country, actually built on words." If this emphasis develops the capacity for immediate and easy friendships, an ability to discuss and debate, and a sense of personal worth, it creates also an insatiable appetite for friends, for signs of personal intimacy, for evidence of social success.[17] The titles of two books about Americans, *The Self-Conscious Society* by Eric Larrabee and *The Lonely Crowd* by David Riesman, capture this paradoxical feature of interpersonal relationships in the United States.

Finally, in the research of the social scientists mentioned earlier there are comparative descriptions of the social attributes of Americans. Abate and Berrien, for example, found Americans high in autonomy, dominance, exhibitionism, affiliation and change.[18] Caudill, in his interpretation of the projective responses of Japanese-Americans and White-Americans found the latter had a warmer, more companionable relationship with parents, encouraged their children to assert themselves more as individuals, were less sensitive to community standards and less vulnerable to external sanctions on their behavior.[19] Similarly, Fenz and Arkoff report considerable contrast between the response patterns of Caucasian and Non-Caucasian groups in Hawaii. Caucasian subjects scored high in dominance, autonomy, aggression, exhibition, achievement, and lowest in deference, nurturance, abasement and order.[20]

Conclusion

The interpersonal attributes of Japanese and Americans appear to be supported by observation, intuition, self-description, other-description, test scores and depth analysis. Specialists in a number of fields, working from different premises and using distinctive methods, seem to concur on many dimensions. The Japanese appear to be more socially vulnerable and to cultivate greater reserve, are more formal and cautious in expressing themselves, communicate less openly and freely. Americans, in contrast, appear more self-assertive and less responsive to social context, are more informal and spontaneous in expressing themselves, and reveal relatively more of their inner experience.

Yet consistency in a cultural profile, though reassuring and in agreement with predictions made here, must not be accepted uncritically. To characterize the style of a culture does not mean that all its members, all the time, in all social circumstances, manifest the same attributes. Nor does it mean that the members of a contrasting culture cannot or do not display similar qualities. Probably the most basic human tendencies are present, in at least latent form, in all peoples. No human beings are completely foreign to each other. Differences between cultures are matters of degree and of relative frequency, not differences of kind.

Further, it is important not to confuse agreement on a cultural profile with the validity of that same profile. The fact that many people share a social stereotype, that they tend to see others in similar ways, does not make them correct. Consensus is suggestive, but it should not be confused with truth. The test of any cultural description is the degree to which it predicts the day-to-day words and actions of the people in that culture. Nevertheless these findings, interesting in themselves, lend considerable support to the cultural models suggested earlier.

All human beings, it appears, enter the world with similar physical potentials, that is, with roughly the same sensory and nervous capabilities. But each culture rapidly undertakes to cultivate a singular set of behavior patterns. By adulthood, and often long before that time, its members begin to display sufficient distinctiveness to permit themselves to be identified as members of a specific culture. However, few people seem to demonstrate such wide contrast in their communicative manner as do Japanese and Americans. And the contrast is sufficiently provocative to encourage further exploration of the actual mechanics of conversation within the two social systems.

4 | Verbal Self Disclosure: Topics, Targets, Depth

Anyone who stands at an urban intersection or in the lobby of a large office building soon senses some pattern in the migrations of people. There are times when they flow together, congregating in dense masses, and times when they disperse and flow apart. Even within such aggregations there are minor currents: some people seek each other out, others meet by accident, and some consciously avoid each other; there are some who never converse, others who speak briefly, and still others who talk at great length.

If we were to look within these encounters we would find further regularities. Conversations usually begin with rituals of greeting. People prolong the relationship, if they desire, through an exchange of prosaic and predictable commonplaces. These conversational pastimes sometimes extend to more serious talk and a deeper sharing of private thought and personal feeling. Each person contributes remarks that will maintain rapport, disclose his experience, and fulfill his needs. From each encounter flows a mixture of consensus or confusion, trust or suspicion, excitement or boredom, affection or animosity.

Probably there are no more basic questions one can ask of a person or a culture than these: To *whom* does one speak or not speak? About *what* may one talk or not talk? How *completely* is inner experience shared or withheld? Answering each of these questions should help to expose the structure of human relationships and the norms that govern interpersonal communication in Japan and the United States.

Person Accessibility

In one of the many insightful cartoon episodes of *Peanuts* Lucy declares, "I love humanity! It's people I can't stand!" And so it is with many human beings. No one seeks to talk to every passerby. No one is a friend to everyone. There is simply not enough time or energy to maintain deep relations with all our neighbors. Nor do most people want to do so.

All people are not equally attractive companions. "Interpersonal valence" is a term that reflects the lines of attraction or rejection that develop among the members of any group or society. Each person and each culture generates criteria for the selection of communicative partners. Any personal quality—age, sex, occupation, education, status, power, talent, beauty—may contribute to or detract from the potential attractiveness of another human being.

What part, if any, do cultures play in the selection of conversational partners? Do Japan and the United States favor communication with the same sorts of people? Are members of one culture closer to their parents, and are members of the other closer to their peers? How do these two societies evaluate conversation with females or males, mothers or fathers, acquaintances or strangers?

Topic Accessibility

How, also, do cultures influence the content of conversations? The catalogue of topics that might be appropriate for conversation is infinite. Yet each person develops his own topical priorities and prejudices, ranking subjects according to their attractiveness to him. Some people prefer to talk about work or family life, others to discuss politics or sex. Some prefer "small talk," enjoying an exchange of information about ordinary daily events, while others prefer "big talk," finding greater stimulation in a discussion of larger philosophical issues.

It would not be surprising to find that people are drawn particularly to those with similar interests. A person who enjoys talking about sports and one who likes to discuss music may not be equally enthralled about meeting an olympic medal winner and a member of a chamber orchestra. If someone—out of ignorance or reticence—is uncomfortable talking about existentialism or birth control, he may simply avoid people who are likely to bring up those subjects.

Cultures not only influence the choice of acquaintances, but mediate also the content of conversation. Each society, to some extent, expresses its values by encouraging or discouraging the exploration of certain subjects. Some topics are approved and freely discussed while others are literally forbidden. A society that attaches great value to business, to the arts, or to family life might be expected to promote somewhat different attitudes toward these areas of discourse. At one time or another in history entire cultures have felt it proper or immoral to discuss religion, sex, evolution, politics, race relations, even dress and diet. Are similar topics approved and disapproved in Japan and the United States? Or do they differ on what is proper and improper for people to talk about?

Every person, within his own circle of acquaintances, also forms different kinds of communicative alliances. Friends are seldom alike in their experience, knowledge, talent, or emotional sensitivity. If this is true, then people may discriminate in what they talk about with each of their acquaintances. Financial matters, for example, may be discussed with parents, but sexual problems only with friends. Or once deep attachments are formed, do people explore without limit any subject that concerns them? Do these two cultures encourage selective communication—limiting the discussion of specific topics to specific target persons—or do they encourage unlimited communication with all associates? If they do support topical discrimination, do both societies favor the same topical priorities with parents, peers, or strangers?

Level Accessibility

There is another dimension to verbal interaction. It has to do with the depth of talk. No matter what topic happens to be in focus, comments may reflect varying degrees of personalization, the extent to which the self is revealed in any remark. A statement may refer to external realities, the outer public world, or to inner realities, the private world inside our skins. Or it may comment on the relations between these two worlds. Remarks of the first type tell very little about the speaker while remarks of the second type tell a great deal more about the person who makes them. Any message, in short, may be highly self disclosing or only slightly self disclosing.

If time were no limitation, every statement could be subjected to this sort of scrutiny. The remark, "You're driving too fast," is a statement about the world outside the self. It claims objective validity. "I get scared going this fast," reflects the inner state of the speaker. The same distinction may be seen in "The company's reorganization plan is sound" compared with "I am excited about my new assignment." The former is a depersonalized judgment, the latter a statement with the self squarely in the center. The mother who says, "The children are going through a difficult phase," and the one who says "I feel inadequate with my children," are conveying quite different information. One tells us about the children, the other about the personal meaning this behavior has for the mother. It reflects her inner experience and informs us as much about her as it does about her children.

In *The Transparent Self* Sidney Jourard emphasizes the difference between people who are "transparent" and those who are "opaque." Some people allow others to know them intimately by often revealing their inner thoughts and feelings, while some hide themselves so others rarely glimpse what they are like inside.[1] Most people, however, are not equally disclosing of themselves on all topics since their emotional comfort and self knowledge are not equal on all topics. They may speak quite frankly on some subjects, those that seem safest, and speak cautiously or deceitfully on subjects that are dangerous. People are not equally honest with all their acquaintances because it is not common to feel equally comfortable with parents, friends, business associates, and complete strangers.

We might expect that cultures, like human beings, would differ in the level of self disclosure they feel is appropriate in conversation. They may prescribe different levels of frankness for different topics: heretical religious views were repressed during the Middle Ages just as firmly as racial doubts remain undiscussed in South Africa today. Societies may differ, also, on the degree of intimacy or distance they feel is appropriate for conversations between people and their parents, their friends, their associates, and strangers. Singular levels and forms of self expression may be cultivated in Japan and the United States.

Self Disclosure Scale

Sidney Jourard and Paul Lasakow have perfected a Self Disclosure Scale which permits simultaneous measurement of three related variables: topic of conversation, target person, and depth of self disclosure.[2] For this study the questionnaire was slightly abridged to reduce its length but without altering its basic structure. The form that was used identified six potential communicative partners: Mother, Father, Same Sex Friend, Opposite Sex Friend, Untrusted Acquaintance, and Stranger. The scale enables one to obtain a picture of the relative intimacy of communicative relationships with six persons who occupy significant places in the interpersonal experience of each respondent.

With each target person the respondent is asked to indicate the level of his or her communication. An appropriate symbol is used to indicate the level of disclosure on a variety of topics with each partner. The symbols and their meanings are as follows: 0—Have told the person nothing about this aspect of myself; 1—Have talked in general terms about this item; 2—Have talked in full and complete detail about this topic; X—Have lied or misrepresented myself to this person. From these scores one can easily calculate the relative accessibility of the self to a variety of other people across a number of conversational topics.

The relative depth of disclosure to these target persons was determined on six broad topics commonly discussed in interpersonal encounters: (1) *Opinions* about political, religious, and social issues, (2) *Interests* in food, music, television, and books, (3) *Work* goals and difficulties, special talents and limitations, (4) *Financial* status, including income, savings, debts, and budget, (5) *Personality*, specific assets and handicaps, sources of pride or shame, (6) *Physical* attributes including feelings about one's face and body, illnesses, sexual adequacy. In each critical area five specific questions sought to fix the location of conversational norms and the limits felt appropriate for each of these general topics. The scales have been used successfully over a period of years to study differences in the disclosure patterns of males and females, members of various races, and people belonging to different cultures.

This questionnaire was given to 120 Japanese and 120 American college students. All were single, were between 18 and 24 years of age, and were equally divided between males and females. Each was asked to read the thirty questions carefully, think of a specific person within each target category (Mother, Father, Same Sex Friend, Opposite Sex Friend, Untrusted Acquaintance, Stranger), and report his actual or probable verbal behavior with each. The tests were completed anonymously, and subjects were given unlimited time to finish.

Topical Priorities

What subjects do members of each of these cultures prefer to talk about, or avoid, when they meet? The answers to this question are somewhat surprising. Instead of a cultural difference in topic preferences, the results revealed immense consistency in what is considered an appropriate or inappropriate topic for conversation.

Among Japanese respondents matters of interest and taste were the most fully discussed topics, followed by opinions about public issues, and attitudes toward work or studies. Financial matters, aspects of personality, and feelings about one's body ranked lower.

Males and females displayed similar topical orientations, although females ranked work-related questions second while males ranked them third. But this difference was slight and insignificant.

American respondents supplied a very similar, but not identical, pattern of response. Matters of taste and interest again scored as the most appealing subjects, but attitudes toward work and studies scored second. Opinions on public issues ranked third, while financial status, aspects of personality, and feelings about physical adequacy followed in that order. But, again, the difference in the relative ranking of attitudes toward work and opinions about public issues was small. And the degree of cultural consistency was very striking. American males and females agreed completely in their topical preferences.

Hence it appears that there are only small and inconsequential differences between Japanese and Americans (and between males and females) with regard to conversational focus: members of both nations seem to prefer to discuss their tastes in food, books, television programs and films, and prefer to talk less about their personal traits and physical or sexual adequacy.

It might be expected that opinions on public issues, since they are the most remote from the self, might be the most favored topics for conversation. But apparently not. Tastes and interests were. There may be several reasons for this. It may be that matters of taste rarely provoke deep or fundamental conflicts in values, and hence are less likely to produce arguments or friction. Or it may be that such differences, since they need not be reconciled, stimulate curiosity rather than animosity. For whatever reason, they constituted the most likely conversational material in both countries.

Scores on the specific questions that make up the six general areas provide further information on verbal disclosure. Among Japanese the most fully explored questions were those relating to tastes in food, music, reading, television and film. Next most fully discussed were opinions on race and male-female relations. The least popular specific questions dealt with feelings about sexual adequacy, facts about sexual behavior, feelings about the appearance of the body and face, and events that arouse shame or guilt. All but the latter two fall into the broad category of attitudes toward the physical self, and the exceptions relate to the adequacy of the psychic self. Males and females differed only slightly in their response even to specific questions on the scale.

Similarly among Americans the most thoroughly explored specific questions concern taste in food, music, television and film, attitudes on race and career goals. Males and females showed only slight differences even with regard to disclosure on specific questions. Americans and Japanese reflected nearly identical patterns of disapproval for conversations relating to personal and sexual matters. And, again, male and female responses revealed no differences sizeable enough to be reliable.

Interestingly the level of talk within each broad area was consistent no matter which specific question was considered. But there was one notable exception to this rule. Questions about sex, for example, appeared under three different topical categories. "My personal opinions about sexual morality" appeared as a question under Opinions on Public Issues, "Facts about my present sex life" appeared under Personality, and "Feelings about my own sexual adequacy" appeared under Physical Attributes. In every case the specific question on sex received the lowest score within the general topic area and, in the last two cases, the lowest scores of any items on the test. This pattern seems to confirm that discussion of the body and its functions is one of the least desirable topics of conversation in both cultures. Sex, even when discussed as a public problem, is seen as a relatively unattractive topic. This may be because it can easily lead to an exploration of attitudes that are highly personal and private. When questions relating to the body and to sexual behavior are set aside, the next lowest specific scores (with the exception of past episodes involving shame or guilt) for both Japanese and Americans referred to money—savings, debts, budgets.

The evidence is overwhelming in support of similar orientations among Japanese and Americans with regard to what is appropriate and inappropriate to talk about. There are slight differences between the cultures on specific questions within the broader categories, but these appear random and inconsequential. Differences between males and females also seem small and, given traditional concepts of their roles, quite understandable.

Target Preferences

If conversational topics can be ranked, is there also a hierarchy of conversational partners? Are the people who occupy our interpersonal worlds equally attractive as associates, or do they vary systematically in attractiveness? Does this change according to topic, or does it remain the same regardless of topic? The data obtained from the Self Disclosure Scale permit these questions to be explored.

A clear hierarchy of target persons emerged from the findings. The Japanese ranked friends highest as communicative partners, parents next, and strangers and untrusted acquaintances last. Within these categories same sex friends were clearly preferred to opposite sex friends, mothers ranked next (scoring nearly as high as friends of the opposite sex), but fathers scored substantially lower. Among the least attractive conversational partners, unknown people were preferred slightly over untrusted acquaintances. While the decline in scores among the most attractive partners (same sex friend, opposite sex friend, mother) was regular, the drop between these and father, stranger, and untrusted person was more precipitous.

All potential target persons scored substantially higher with Americans, but essentially the same hierarchy existed. Friends were communicated with most fully, parents next, and strangers and untrusted people least. Also, the scores decreased gradually and a radical drop did not appear until one reaches the scores for strangers and untrusted people. Again, unknown persons were preferred to untrusted ones.

There are some interesting, though subtle and unreliable, differences in the responses of males and females in both samples. Japanese males appeared to disclose most to male friends, but more fully to friends of either sex than to their mothers. Japanese females disclosed most to the same sex friend, but next to their mothers. There was substantial disclosure to opposite sex friends, but it was less complete than to mothers. Americans, both male and female, communicated more fully with friends of either sex than they did with either parent.

Verbal disclosure to fathers may differ in the two cultures: Americans appeared to communicate almost equally with mothers and fathers; Japanese seemed to differentiate between the amount of disclosure with each parent. Whereas disclosure to American fathers was nearly indistinguishable from other intimates, disclosure to Japanese fathers dropped off considerably and approaches the level of American disclosure with strangers. Americans revealed more of themselves to strangers and untrusted associates, but, like the Japanese, preferred the former to the latter as communicative partners.

Choice of topic and choice of partner would not seem to be independent of each other. They should interact. It would seem reasonable that most people would seek out specific persons when they wish to discuss certain topics, and seek other partners to discuss other topics. But the data from this investigation raise doubts about that presumption, for there was considerable consistency across all topics for all target persons. That is to say, there was little evidence of either avoidance of or emphasis upon particular topics with particular acquaintances. Generally tastes and opinions were the most fully discussed in both cultures with all people. And physical attributes and personal traits were the least discussed, again with all people.

These generalizations may obscure some exceptions to this rule. Some Japanese respondents, for example, seemed to prefer to discuss financial matters with their mothers, next with male friends and female friends. They preferred to talk about bodily characteristics, excepting sexual behavior, with mothers before male or female friends. Among Americans, financial matters seemed more likely to be discussed with mothers, secondly with fathers, rather than with peers of the same or opposite sex. Unlike their Japanese counterparts, Americans did not appear to find discussion of physical attributes easier with mothers or fathers than with the same or opposite sex friend. But evidence of selective communication is too haphazard to be taken seriously.

Thus it appears there is a communicative bias operating in both countries that encourages greater personal disclosure to same and opposite sex friends, favors somewhat less disclosure to parents, and restricts interaction still more with unknown and untrusted people. Each sex seems somewhat to prefer communicating with members of the same sex, but this preference is much stronger among Japanese than Americans. The Japanese seem to differentiate more sharply between communicating with mothers and fathers while Americans seem to perceive both parents as more equally attractive partners.

Level of Personal Involvement

The order of topical priorities and hierarchy of communicative partners seem generally consistent in both cultures. But what is most critical is the depth of personal disclosure that is encouraged within interpersonal encounters. How much of themselves do Japanese and Americans reveal in their conversations? The data obtained from the Self Disclosure Scale provide a simple and clear index of self revelation.

The scoring of the Self Disclosure Scale is such that a score of 0 indicates that respondents "Have told nothing about this aspect of myself," a score of 100 indicates they "Have talked in general terms about this aspect of myself," and a score of 200 indicates they "Have talked in full and complete detail about this item."* Scores falling between 0–100 would suggest a low level and between 100–200 a high level of self disclosure. With so broad a range of topics and so diverse a set of communicative partners it would be surprising if scores averaged above 150.

For the Japanese the average level of disclosure across all topics and all target persons was 75. The average disclosure score for Americans was 112. Scores of males and females in both cultures were very similar: Japanese males and females obtained exactly the same scores on self revelation; Americans showed a slight sex difference, males averaging 113 and females averaging 110. (The small differences in disclosure levels of American males and females is traceable to relatively greater openness of males with

---

*To simplify the presentation of the results on the Self Disclosure Scale raw scores have been multiplied by 100 to convert them into whole numbers.

strangers.) But these differences were so small they cannot be taken very seriously.

However, it may be more representative of a culture to consider the level of communication only with "trusted acquaintances." Although conversations with strangers may be suggestive of the range of social interaction it seems questionable to incorporate this figure in appraising the general level of disclosure in daily conversation. Disclosure to untrusted people, too, seems to constitute a special rather than typical instance of personal interaction. A better and more representative estimate of the normal depth of disclosure may be secured by eliminating these two categories of target persons.

When these are omitted from the calculations, the average level of conversation with trusted acquaintances (mother, father, male friend, female friend) rises from 75 to 100 for the Japanese and from 112 to 144 for Americans. A slight sex difference appeared in both samples, but again of such small size as to be discounted.

With regard to overall levels of interpersonal communication the findings seem clear. Interpersonal distance, as estimated by self disclosure, was substantially greater among Japanese than among Americans. The degree to which persons shared their experience—private opinion and private feeling—was considerably higher among Americans. And this appeared to be true whether potential partners included or excluded unknown and untrusted persons.

For Japanese the average level of disclosure rose to 100 only with trusted acquaintances. This indicates, on the average, that Japanese express themselves only "in general terms" with their closest associates—parents and intimate friends. For the United States the comparable figure was 144. While this figure does not suggest a total sharing of the self, it does indicate a level of expression that varies between talking "in general terms" and talking "in full and complete detail about oneself." In order to reach this level approximately half of all communication with intimates would have to involve a full sharing of the self.

The precise boundaries of the "public self" and the "private self" in Japan and the United States may now be estimated using the data on self disclosure. The generalized models suggested earlier can now be drawn more precisely. (These appear in Figures 11 and 12.) In the typical Japanese the area of the "private self" extends from the "unconscious" to the point at which the person reveals his inner feelings in only "general terms" (100). For the typical American the "private self" extends from the "unconscious" to a point midway between disclosing his inner experience "completely" or in "general terms" (144). Thus the total area of the self accessible to others through communication is significantly smaller in Japan than in the United States. (It is possible to represent the boundary of the public and private self in each topical area—for a culture or an individual—by making the contour of this boundary conform precisely to the profile of scores in each topical area and for each conversational partner.)

Figure 11   Precise Boundary of Public Self

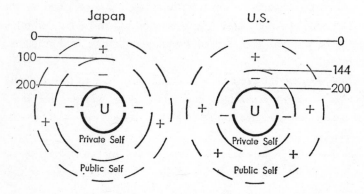

It is when individual questionnaires are examined that the full impact of these findings is felt. Depersonalized averages tend to obscure extreme cases and blunt somewhat the human significance of these overall figures. Many people reported no disclosure of self on a number of topics; many others reported no instances of deep disclosure to any person. There were more than a few, especially among the Japanese sample, whose average level of self expression was not near 100, but closer to 0, who on *nearly all topics* and with *nearly all people* reported they "Have told the person nothing about this aspect of myself." As one data processor remarked while scoring some of the questionnaires, "Have these people ever revealed anything about themselves to anyone? Are they known to any other human being at all?" This is a stronger indictment of Japanese conversational manner than that offered by Robert Guillain, but it is similar in tone. He notes that the Japanese enjoy social contacts, but contacts that are more pleasant than deep: "Beyond polite phrases, the Japanese speaks very little, particularly about himself."[3]

The avoidance of frank or full disclosure of interior experience is reflected not only in the findings of this study but in many commentaries on social behavior in Japan. James Moloney, for example, remarks that "There are vast areas of behavior about which the ordinary Japanese may be unwilling to talk freely."[4] Conversation, according to Bernard Krisher, is founded on an "economy of words," with couples often spending a lifetime together without ever discussing their feelings with one another.[5] There appears to be strong cultural resistance to excessive verbalization and a compensating reverencing of silence and less explicit forms of expression. Many Japanese aphorisms reflect this cultural attitude. Talkative persons, for example, are characterized as resembling a "paper carp in May." Like these inflated banners, talkative people consist only of huge open mouths with nothing but air inside.

If verbal disclosure among Japanese is restricted, and is consistent with cultural attributes such as "reserved," "cautious," "evasive," and "silent," so is the extent of verbal expression among Americans more uninhibited and equally consistent with cultural traits such as "talkative," "frank," and "self assertive." If one society favors a "restrained self," the other favors an "unrestrained self"; where one encourages "contraction," the other encourages "expansion." Those in the United States who are inarticulate, verbally vague or clumsy with words, and those unwilling to contribute or express their views, have limited influence. Status and respect are accorded people with unusual capacity for defining problems and mobilizing support for their solution. An appetite or aptitude for expressing the self verbally seems differently valued in these two cultures.

Level of Disclosure by Topic

Interpersonal encounters move through a more or less patterned sequence. People talk first in more formal ways. The subject matter is more distant than self-revealing (Tastes). Gradually, after an appropriate period of exploratory testing, conversants move to more personal levels of talk (Opinions, Work). Finally, as mutual trust grows between them, they may drop their defenses and exchange more private feelings (Personal and Physical). Not only does the topical focus change with time, but also the level of disclosure deepens on each topic. If so, the findings of this study suggest that among Japanese this is often an incomplete process, the topical progression is interrupted earlier and is less often carried to the point of deep mutual sharing. Though the same overall pattern undoubtedly appears in American conversations, they seem to move more quickly and more consistently to the final stages. Clearly neither culture always completes this process; each favors some restriction upon the sharing of inner meanings.

The average level of verbal disclosure can easily be computed for each topical area. The figures presented in Table 1 reinforce the earlier conclusion drawn from overall averages. Americans showed a consistently higher level of self revelation on all topics. In fact, their level of disclosure on the least appealing topic in both cultures equaled or surpassed the level of disclosure of Japanese on all but the most preferred topic. That is, Americans shared nearly as much of themselves with regard to physical and sexual adequacy as the Japanese did with regard to their preferences in food, music, reading materials and television programs.

Table 1   Average Disclosure on Conversational Topics

	Japanese	American
Average Disclosure on All Topics (To All Persons)	75	112
Average Disclosure on All Topics (To Intimates)	100	144
Average Disclosure by Topic (To Intimates):		
Interests/Tastes	126	163
Work/Studies	113	162
Opinions on Public Issues	107	151
Financial	96	143
Personality	90	129
Physical	69	113

Again, individual patterns of communication within specific topics were revealing, and convey some of the uniqueness of the responses. What often appeared among both Americans and Japanese might be called "communicative blanks." Though most respondents talked with some intimacy to some people on some topics, there were areas of private experience that were blotted out completely. Some, for example, avoided discussing illness or debts or sex with anyone, while others avoided conversations that touched upon race relations or Communism or work handicaps. (Somewhat surprising was the finding that Americans disclosed slightly more to each other on the subject of sexual standards than on the subject of Communism.) It seems, then, that some people confine interaction to well-worn conversational ruts, often avoiding alternative topical material. Both healthy and symptomatic communicative patterns may be identifiable in these individual profiles of self disclosure.

Level of Disclosure to Significant Persons

Finally, we may examine the relation between levels of disclosure and the persons with whom one converses. As noted earlier, both countries tended to rank potential communicative partners in similar ways. The precise averages for disclosure to all target persons, trusted target persons, and each of the specific persons identified in this study are presented in Table 2.

Table 2 Average Disclosure to Target Persons

	Japanese	American
Average Disclosure to All Partners (All Topics)	75	112
Average Disclosure to Intimates (All Topics)	100	144
Average Disclosure to Specific Target Persons:		
Same Sex Friend	122	157
Opposite Sex Friend	103	153
Mother	100	138
Father	75	126
Stranger	27	58
Untrusted Acquaintance	22	38

Again, the overall level of disclosure, regardless of whether all target persons or only trusted ones are included, was substantially lower among the Japanese than among the Americans. On the whole, the Japanese talked only in the most general terms even with their own parents and closest friends. The overall average for Americans with all target persons, including unknown and untrusted people, exceeded the level of personal exchange of Japanese in even their most intimate relationships. The figures for specific target persons, of course, elaborated this general trend. The extent of personal disclosure for the Japanese was roughly similar for male friend, female friend and mother, but then dropped sharply. For Americans the communication levels with male friend and female friend were nearly identical, and similar for father and mother. The level dropped more sharply only with strangers and untrusted people.

Yet it is important not to overlook the diversity that lies behind cultural norms. In both samples there were some who communicated deeply with their mothers, but others who communicated with them superficially. If some discussed a wide set of topics with their closest friends, there were others who were more discriminating about what they talk about with their same or opposite sex friends. Where some did not explore any topic with strangers in depth, others appeared to be more open with strangers than with their own parents. Still, despite such individual variability, the consistency within each cultural group was striking and the contrast between them was substantial.

Disclosure to Fathers

Disclosure to fathers appeared to constitute a special instance of interpersonal communication. According to Jourard there is less sharing of the self with fathers than with mothers and peers in many cultures. If so, our data did not confirm that conclusion among Americans, but strongly reinforced that generalization among Japanese. There was substantially less disclosure to fathers than to any other intimate associates inside or outside the family. Americans apparently shared their private thoughts and feelings nearly as much with strangers as Japanese did with their own fathers. These findings tend to substantiate the saying that there are four things Japanese fear most: earthquakes, thunder, fire, and fathers. The inclusion of fathers on a list of purely physical occurrences appears to be more than accidental. At any rate the evidence supports Benedict's characterization of Japanese fathers as "depersonalized objects" and Doi's description of Japan as a "fatherless society."

A study of the communicative orientations of high school students corroborates these results. With regard to the question "With whom can you share your troubles most freely and frankly?" Japanese students ranked in order of attractiveness "mothers," "intimate friends," "older brothers and sisters," "younger brothers and sisters," and "fathers." When asked to identify the person with whom they shared the least communicatively, fathers were the nearly unanimous choice. These students reported saying little to their fathers beyond "Good morning" and "Goodnight." In contrast, mothers were the persons with whom the most was shared conversationally.[6]

When asked to identify the chief role of their father among those of "Friend," "Teacher," "Advisor," "Boss," "Partner," or "None of these," Japanese college students rarely chose "Friend." Many found none of the terms really suitable in describing his role. Among those who did, most preferred "Boss" or "Advisor." Only 11% regarded him as a "Friend."[7] Hiroyoshi Ishikawa reports a similar sentiment reflected in college students' perceptions of their fathers. They described him as "alone" or "isolated," a remote figure surrounded by forbidding walls that reduced conversation to commonplaces.[8]

Conclusion

Conversation is an activity sustained by two or more persons who use their private experience as a resource on which to build some sort of human relationship. The kind of relationship, of course, depends on their desire and capacity to maintain a deep or shallow linkage with each other. The findings of this study, reflected in the accompanying visual summary, suggest there is both universality and distinctiveness in the verbal style cultivated in each culture. (Comparisons along any dimension can be made simply be glancing down the columns to compare the extent of disclosure with each communicative partner, or across the rows to contrast the level of disclosure on each topic.)

These charts reveal that both cultures cultivate a similar set of attitudes toward people who are the potential receivers of messages. As communicative partners, peers are preferred to parents, parents are preferred to strangers. Within these categories there is a slight preference for same sex over opposite sex friends, but a more marked preference, especially in Japan, for mothers over fathers. Neither culture encourages verbal intimacy with strangers. Both societies also promote similar orientations toward a wide range of topics. In both, people tend to talk more about their tastes, opinions, and work than about their financial affairs, personal traits, and physical or sexual adequacy.

But here the similarity ends. These two countries appear to differ sharply in the depth of conversation they feel is appropriate in interpersonal encounters. Among Japanese there is substantially less disclosure of inner experience while among Americans

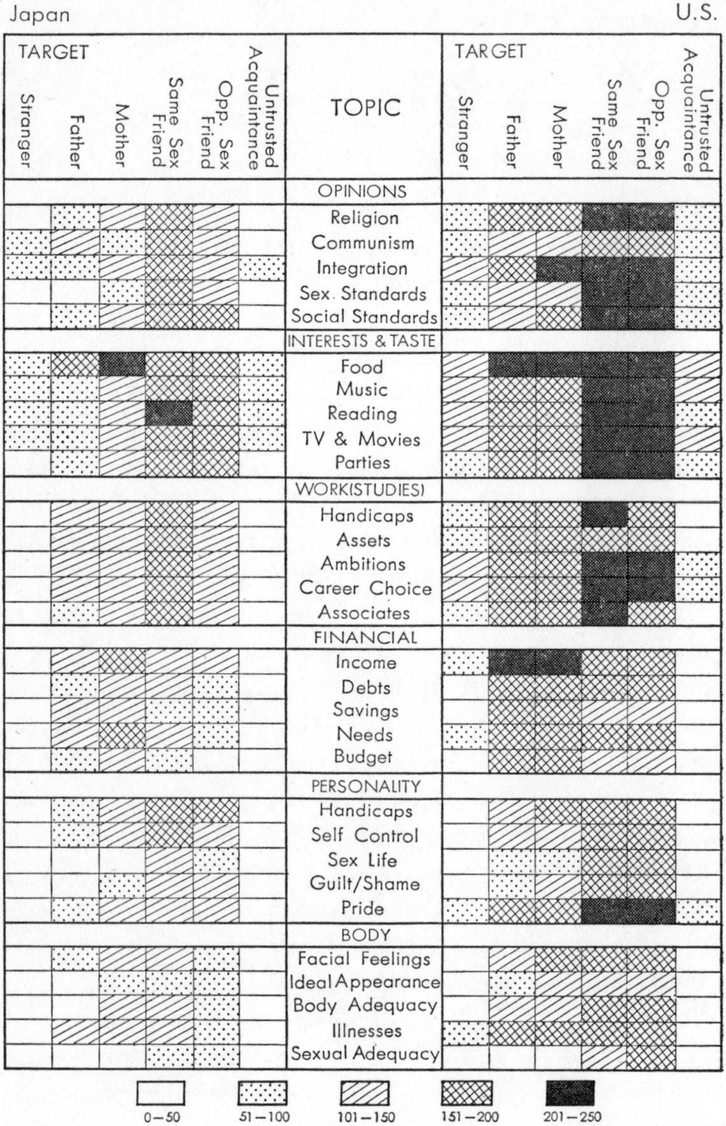

Figure 12   Summary of Topic, Target, and Level of Disclosure

substantially greater disclosure on all topics and with all persons. Where the former share their private thoughts in only a general way, among the latter these are revealed much more completely. Americans, for example, reveal themselves more completely on the most superficially explored topics than do the Japanese on all but the safest and most completely explored topics of conversation. Other studies seem to confirm that many conversations among the Japanese, even among members of the family, chiefly concern matters of taste.

This discrepancy in verbal disclosure appears both as a cause and consequence of cultural values. Speech, to many Japanese, is not a highly regarded form of communication. Words are often discounted or viewed with suspicion. Talk is disparaged. It is realities, not words, that regulate human affairs. Sayings such as "By your mouth you shall perish" reflect this basic mistrust of language as a vehicle of communication. In the words of Inazo Nitobe, "To give in so many articulate words one's innermost thoughts and feelings is taken among us as an unmistakable sign that they are neither profound nor very sincere."[9] This thought is put more bluntly still by Hidetoshi Kato when he says, "In Japan speech is not silver or copper or brass—but scrap."[10] Intuitive communication, through means other than words, is praised and revered. Articulate persons, especially talkative ones, are seen as foolish or even dangerous. Eloquence can even disqualify one for positions of authority or influence.

In contrast, among Americans the ability to articulate ideas and feelings is highly respected. Speech is seen not only as the species differentiating potential of human beings, but the source of their greatest accomplishment as well. The social system rests upon a deep commitment to discussion as the primary mode of inquiry, of learning, of negotiation, and of decision making. Valued ideals and critical procedures are nearly always codified in constitutions and contracts in order to clarify them and to minimize misunderstanding. An ability to define problems and to formulate solutions to them is a highly prized and even an indispensable social skill. Words are regarded as the principal vehicle for preserving human contact, the most sensitive and flexible means of transmitting experience.

In any case, the character of verbal disclosure in the two cultures provides support for the original hypothesis: Japanese and Americans differ in the degree to which the self is exposed and accessible in interpersonal encounters. The "public self" as distinguished from the "private self" constitutes a smaller area of the total self among Japanese and a larger area among Americans.

There are further questions to which these findings point, and some which the reader may already be asking: What are the personal and social consequences of this difference? Does fuller expression stimulate growth or does it impair it? Are the dangers of overexposure as great as those of underexposure? Is someone capable of communicating at deeper levels likely to communicate better interpersonally or interculturally? These questions can be explored but first it would be helpful to know more of the character of nonverbal interaction and of the prevailing forms of defensive communication in these two cultures.

5 | Nonverbal Self Disclosure: Touchables and Untouchables

The earliest form of contact with the world is through touch. Even our sense of personal identity originates in a physical communication. As the infant touches his hands and feet, gradually exploring the boundaries of his own body, he begins to recognize and accept his separate existence. There is a constant flow of affection and hostility between infant and mother long before a child can talk about what he experiences. During this period physical cues are his principal source of information and his most eloquent means of personal expression. Touch is the primary means by which a human being establishes his first and most critical human relationship.

"There is a general embryological law," writes Ashley Montagu, "that the earlier a function develops the more fundamental it is likely to be."[1] He is not alone in this view. For this reason many psychologists regard touch as the primary channel of human communication, and the base on which all other senses rest. Verbal messages, it is argued, are no more than substitutes for physical ones. One psychiatrist refers to words as replacements for stroking.

Even in adulthood physical touch is so powerful a means of personal revelation that often, in spite of the presence of accompanying words, it overrides all other message cues.

The skin is not only the most extensive organ system of the body, it is, as well, one with the widest range of sensitivity. Space and time can be handled as well, or better, through stimulation of the surface of the body than through the ear or eye. The number of sensory fibers carrying information from the skin to the spinal cord exceeds the number from any other organ of the body. The surface of the body may easily constitute the largest and most potent channel of all for carrying interpersonal messages.

Studies of infant behavior, both animal and human, reveal how critical physical contact is in the evolution of a healthy adult. Gentled infants, in contrast to those who have rarely been touched or caressed, show greater gain in weight, higher level of activity, greater curiosity and capacity for learning, withstand physical illness and psychological stress better, and survive longest. Without such handling the infant may suffer from physical limitations, mental retardation, emotional disturbance, and social inadequacy. Tactile communication, at least during infancy, appears a decisive and essential experience for optimal physical and social maturation. Without it the infant may not survive at all, or may survive hampered by an inability to respond adequately to the surrounding physical and social world.

Even among adults a vast range of meaning can be conveyed through physical contact alone. The ultimate hostile act is, of course, a physical one. But so, also, is the ultimate intimacy. Fighting and sexual intercourse represent only the extremes on a scale of expressiveness that includes an infinity of subtle feelings. It is a rare verbal message that is not accompanied by some form of gestural commentary. Actions, in many instances, do speak louder than words. And touch may well be the most potent action of all. Its impact, because of early infant dependence upon it, may exceed that of all other communicative cues.

Further, it appears more difficult to dissemble and deceive physically than verbally. A forced intimacy or ritualized embrace is difficult to bring off without revealing the lack of spontaneity behind it. Many physical attributes, such as muscular tension and skin temperature, are under unconscious rather than conscious control, so people may hesitate to express themselves through touch if their feelings are less than genuine.

The mere frequency of physical contact appears to be a sensitive barometer of interpersonal closeness. Enemies rarely approach one another, and any contact is likely to be restricted to hostile acts. Strangers, too, usually stand at some distance from each other, avoiding all but prescribed and ritualized forms of physical touch. Among acquaintances one usually notices somewhat greater ease and spontaneity, and close friends are often visually identifiable because of their physical responsiveness to each other. They stand close together, bodies often touching, and more often tug, clasp, pat, and caress one another. The more comfortable people are with each other—the more willing they are to be known to each other—the more one can expect them to communicate by physical as well as verbal means.

Both codes, verbal and nonverbal, must be mastered of course to permit full and flexible human interaction. There are meanings that can only be shared verbally, and others that can only be shared nonverbally. It would be as awkward and ineffective to dance a constitution as it would be to attempt a verbal embrace. If there are truths that can only be stated, there are others that can only be conveyed through human contact. Sometimes in interpersonal encounters people succeed verbally while failing miserably in a nonverbal sense. Liza Doolittle in *My Fair Lady*, thoroughly exasperated with Freddy, her naive and wordy admirer, cries out: "Don't *talk* of love. Show me!"

Nonverbal Codes and Cultures

Toward so potent a form of self disclosure cultures adopt radically different attitudes. A surprising number of the most sensitive norms of every culture regulate whom one can touch, when one can touch, and what one can touch. Just as an infant learns not to put everything into its mouth, it learns not to let everything out of its mouth. There are things to say and things not to say. Similarly, there are things one can do and cannot do with inclinations to touch or be touched. Holding hands is encouraged in some cultures, but is ridiculed in others; patting the head is an expression of intimacy in some societies, but can be a fatal gesture in others. No matter what the young infant may be prompted to express physically, he is trained to channel these impulses into culturally acceptable forms of expression.

It should be emphasized that to assimilate these codes, the nonverbal as well as the verbal, is an absolute necessity for survival. It is indispensable to the achievement of individual identity and to the realization of personal potentials; it is prerequisite to membership and effectiveness in the human community. No human beings can share any meaning at all unless they create a channel and a common code for transmitting it. Repeated violations of the cultural codes that mediate communication lead as inevitably to confusion and conflict as do infractions of traffic rules contribute to automobile accidents. Misunderstanding is an inevitable consequence of communicative negligence, of insensitive or accidental violations of the rules of meaning. Yet in assimilating such codes each person learns also to repress or redirect certain impulses. Later it may not only be awkward to use the nonverbal forms of another culture, it may be difficult even to recognize that such impulses for physical expression exist within him.

Casual observation would lead to the suspicion that persons raised in Japan and the United States are exposed both to similar and to different rules regarding physical contact. In both countries one finds great intimacy between mother and infant during the first months of life. In Japan a greater physical distance soon begins to separate the infant and its father; American children do not seem to differentiate as sharply between their physical behavior with their parents. Still greater contrast appears between the cultures with regard to strangers; where American children often interact freely with strangers, Japanese children appear indifferent to or fearful of them.

During early schooling there is considerable physical contact within sex groupings in both countries. Physical play and physical aggression appear in both, though the incidence of affectionate display may be higher between girls and between boys in Japan than in the United States. Prior to adolescence greater sexual exclusiveness develops in both cultures, but in Japan this is reinforced by more differentiated role treatment and, in some instances, by segregated education. Physical displays of affection continue in Japan (walking arm and arm or hand in hand), while in the United States such intimacy diminishes between girls and usually disappears between American boys.

In adolescence the pattern changes once more. In both countries physical contact declines further between members of the same sex, but such contact appears to diminish more sharply in the United States. There is, however, increasing physical intimacy between males and females in the United States, but minimal physical contact between the sexes in Japan. While there are occasional displays of physical intimacy in Japan, mutual acts such as embracing or kissing are rare in public. This pattern of physical contact within sex groupings combined with severely limited interaction between the sexes continues in Japan into college and beyond.

Yet this pattern is violated in at least one instance. In the company of strangers Japanese often display indifference to physical contact and even considerable aggressiveness. In moving through crowds of strangers or forcing their way onto loaded subway cars the Japanese show little irritation over violations of personal space that often upset Westerners considerably. Thus an aversion to most types of physical intimacy between acquaintances contrasts with striking casualness about physical contact in the company of strangers.

Despite some overall similarity in the patterns of physical interaction that mark the stages from infancy to maturity in both countries, there is reason to expect some differences in the form, the frequency, and the significance of touch as a form of communication. Sleeping patterns within the family, for one, contrast sharply. Members of Japanese families sleep together, rather than apart, for most of their lives. A recent study of more than three hundred households in Tokyo, Kyoto and Matsumoto revealed that sleeping together was still the dominant pattern from infancy until adolescence, and again from marriage until old age. This physical closeness, according to the investigators, cultivates an increasing interdependence among family members in contrast to the independence encouraged by separate sleeping arrangements in American families. While lack of space might account for this pattern among the Japanese, physical crowding was not found to be a critical factor.[2] Other investigators, too, report that familial sleeping patterns are preferred and welcomed rather than being matters of necessity.[3]

More significant still may be differences in the patterns of mothering in the two countries. At no time is the human personality as malleable, as totally dependent upon signals from others, as during infancy. At birth a child must rely exclusively upon touch as its singular link with the outside world. Even as other senses mature the skin remains a primary source of information. During these early months, before the capacity for speech develops, an infant forms its view of the world, its orientation toward people, its characteristic manner of expression. The character of nonverbal communication with infants—particularly the amount and quality of physical contact—affects physical growth, mental alertness, emotional responsiveness and social effectiveness. The persistence of cultural identities in the face of technological homogenization is traceable to this source: the most critical determinants of personality, and those most resistant to change, are found in patterns of infant care. Socilaization occurs in the early weeks of life, and this means socialization to a specific cultural pattern.

Such an effort to identify the distinctive features of socialization in Japan and the United States has been carried out. Two investigators, Caudill and Weinstein, carefully recorded the interaction between thirty sets of infants and mothers, both Japanese and American. In general they found that Japanese mothers spent more time with their infants, emphasized physical over verbal interaction, and encouraged the development of a passive, contented child. In contrast, American mothers spent less time with their infants, interacted verbally more than through touch, and seemed to cultivate a more active and assertive child. Culture, they noted, is the most important source of differences in the infants they observed, producing distinguishable patterns of behavior within a few months after birth.[4]

All of this might suggest that the Japanese, who appear to discourage verbalization, might encourage nonverbalization. Is this the case? Do Americans, since they talk more, limit the use of physical contact as a channel of communication? Do Japanese, since they talk less, express more through the medium of touch? This would seem a reasonable expectation, but is it correct?

The Nonverbal Inventory

The object in this phase of the study was to substitute hard fact for impressionistic description, to determine more precisely and more objectively the character of nonverbal interaction in Japan and the United States. How frequently do members of the two cultures touch each other? Whom do they touch? What areas of the body are involved in such contacts? And what, if any, differences in physical expression characterize the communicative styles of males and females with regard to touching behavior?

Since Americans have already been described as spontaneous, informal, and assertive—and have already been found more willing to disclose themselves verbally—what can we expect of them nonverbally? What might be predicted for the Japanese who have been described as formal, reserved, evasive, distant—and who have been found to be less expressive verbally?

It is possible that people who are verbally expressive have less need to be so nonverbally. Ability to communicate inner feelings and thoughts through words might substitute for sharing them through actions. Or, conversely, restrictions on verbal expression might increase the need for alternative channels of communication.

But with equal persuasiveness it could be argued that the need to express the inner self knows no limitations. That one who feels or thinks deeply and is eager to share these reactions will employ every available means. And that someone who has learned to inhibit his expression, or who feels less urge to share inner experience with others, may be as unwilling to employ nonverbal channels as he is verbal ones. These questions may be clarified by examining

Figure 13   Nonverbal Inventory Diagram

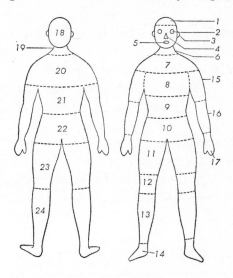

the character of nonverbal contact in the two cultures.

The Nonverbal Inventory used to collect information on cultural habits of interpersonal contact was adapted from Jourard's Body Accessibility Questionnaire.[5] Earlier work with this scale demonstrated that it measures physical contact sensitively and reliably. It was given to 240 college students divided equally between Japanese and Americans, males and females. All respondents were unmarried and between the ages of 18 and 24.

Each person was asked to examine two diagrams which reproduced a front and rear view of the human body. (See Figure 13.) Each figure, undifferentiated as to sex, was sectioned into twenty-four areas and each of these was identified by number. To reduce errors of recall and to eliminate childhood behavior, all were asked to consider only nonverbal contacts since the age of fourteen. Accidental physical contact and contact resulting from participation in sports were also to be omitted from consideration. Thus only deliberate communicative acts and the specific area of contact were to be reported. Each person was asked to indicate both where they had "touched" or been "touched by" father, mother, same sex friend, and opposite sex friend. The forms were completed anonymously and the instructions emphasized that "There are no right or wrong answers, only honest or dishonest ones." All questionnaires appeared to be completed carefully and accurately.

The results secured from the Nonverbal Inventory should reveal the relative physical accessibility of persons in each culture, areas of the body that are touched or avoided, and any differences between male and female patterns of touching.

Nonverbal Contact: What is Touched?

With regard to parts of the body that are touched, there was evidence of a sharp differentiation between areas of frequent contact and those of rare contact. There was, also, almost total agreement between the cultures on areas of the body that can be touched and those that should not be touched. Among the Japanese the most frequently reported areas of contact were the hand, shoulder, forehead, back of neck and head, and forearm. Among Americans the same results obtained except for the addition of the upper arm. The areas of physical avoidance showed similar agreement: in both cultures the front pelvic region, rear pelvic region, rear thigh and rear lower leg were rarely touched. Although some areas of physical avoidance may reflect inconvenience rather than inhibition, both cultures seem to differentiate sharply between the parts of the body that are legitimate and illegitimate channels of nonverbal communication.

Nonverbal Contact: Who is Touched?

When total physical contact with others is considered, Japanese and Americans showed their highest frequency of touching behavior to be with friends rather than with parents. But these overall totals mask some differences within the categories of target persons.

Japanese, for example, reported their greatest physical contact with opposite sex friends, next with mothers and same sex friends (with almost no differentiation between them), then a drop-off in contact with fathers. Americans showed a similar profile with their greatest physical contact with opposite sex friends, next with mothers, next with same sex friends, and finally with fathers. But opposite sex friends scored much higher with Americans as desirable recipients of nonverbal contact, and fathers ranked very close to same sex friends.

Although both cultures regarded opposite sex friends as the most desirable and fathers as the least desirable communicative partners with regard to physical contact, they differed markedly in the degree of differentiation. Where the Japanese treated opposite sex friends as only somewhat more attractive than mothers or same sex friends, Americans treated them as considerably more attractive. Where Americans showed nearly the same degree of physical intimacy with fathers that they manifest with same sex friends, the Japanese interacted noticeably less with fathers than with any other target person.

Nonverbal Contact: Touching and Touched

The Nonverbal Inventory distinguishes between "touching" (initiating physical contact) and "being touched" (being the recipient of physical contact). Yet when these two behaviors were compared the frequency of "touching" and of "being touched" appeared to increase or decrease together. If the score on one was high, so was the score on the other. Both cultures retained the same overall ranking of target areas and target persons on both dimensions. There was remarkable consistency in the two patterns, although "being touched" was reported slightly more often than "touching." Apparently the desire to initiate and the desire to receive meanings through physical contact atrophy or ripen together. At least this is the pattern reflected in the responses of members of these two cultures.

Nonverbal Contact: Male and Female

Do men and women observe similar or different norms concerning physical accessibility and, if so, are these the same for both cultures or do they differ?

Males and females in both countries appeared to prefer physical contact with friends over physical contact with parents, at least by early adulthood. Opposite sex friends consistently scored the highest and fathers consistently scored the lowest on physical intimacy regardless of sex or culture. Yet there were some variations in the touching patterns of males and females.

Male respondents in both cultures reported their closest contact with opposite sex friends, next with same sex friends, next with mothers, and finally with fathers. But for American males opposite sex friends ranked substantially higher while there was less differentiation among other target persons. Japanese males, although they exhibited the same overall ranking of significant other persons differentiated less between opposite sex friends and other target figures.

Female respondents in both cultures gave a somewhat different pattern of reponse. Like their male counterparts, they reported their greatest contact with opposite sex friends, but ranked their mothers second. Same sex friends and fathers followed in that order. Again, American women showed a marked preference for opposite sex friends over other target persons; Japanese women, in contrast, differentiated less among associates except for scoring fathers lower on the scale.

There are a number of implications contained in these findings. The evidence suggests that cultural differences exert a stronger influence than sexual differences. Research on infant behavior has already shown culture to be more powerful than sex in shaping the early behavior of infants. The findings here suggest that even in early adulthood culture remains a more potent influence than sex in determining the character of human interaction.

There is also some suggestion of a difference in cultural attitudes toward the same and opposite sex. Although both cultures clearly preferred to interact with the opposite sex, Americans showed a strong preference for contact with opposite sex friends while Japanese showed no such favoritism among target persons. Among Americans, contact with the opposite sex was reported nearly twice as often as with the same sex while among the Japanese the difference was much smaller. This might suggest there is greater closeness and comfort within sex boundaries in Japan and somewhat greater closeness and comfort across sex lines in the United States. Although casual observation might support such a conclusion, the evidence of this study is not sufficient on this point.

In both countries females reported "being touched" slightly more than "touching," while males reported slightly more "touching" than "being touched." Conceivably such a difference might document male initiative in heterosexual relations, but the difference is not large enough to support such a conclusion.

The last finding that deserves elaboration concerns interaction with fathers. In both cultures they scored as the person with whom there is the least physical contact. The data suggested that Americans are nearly as close to their fathers as their mothers. Among Japanese the gulf appeared to be wider. Japanese males ranked their fathers lowest in physical contact, but showed no sharp drop in contact with them compared to other intimates. Japanese females, however, not only ranked their fathers substantially below all others but reported only half as much contact with them as with mothers, and considerably less even than with same sex friends. The physical isolation of fathers in Japan, thus, appears to parallel their verbal isolation. Research has shown that people stand closer to and touch more often people they feel affection for; they stand farther from and touch less often those they dislike or fear. If so, the evidence on physical contact between Japanese and their fathers would suggest either a much lower or perhaps fearfully high regard for them. Not only do our respondents appear to disclose little of themselves to their fathers through conversation; they communicate equally little of themselves by means of physical contact.

Although extensive physical communication may take place between children and parents, in adulthoood the larger proportion of touching behavior is directed toward peers. While both societies share a preference for contact with friends over parents, there are cultural nuances within these patterns: where Japanese distinguished sharply between parental figures, favoring mothers over fathers, Americans tended to treat both parents alike with regard to touching behavior. With peers the opposite picture obtained, the Japanese treating opposite sex friends more alike and Americans treating them much more distinctively.

Nonverbal Contact: Extent of Touching Behavior

So far the comparisons have been internal ones. That is they have focused mainly on distinctions within each culture—between touching and being touched, between one area of the body and another, between male and female initiative, between parents and peers as recipients of communication through touch.

But the sharpest contrast appears when the general level of accessibility is considered across cultures. Here the scores provide a picture of dramatic contrast. In nearly every category, whether one focuses on an area of the body or a communicative partner, the amount of physical contact reported by Americans is nearly twice that reported by Japanese. As a channel of interpersonal communication touch appears to be nearly twice as important within one culture as within the other.

Americans reported 50% greater contact with their mothers, and reported more than twice the amount of contact with their fathers as do the Japanese. Americans appeared also to engage in twice as much contact with their friends as do the Japanese. While the difference between the cultures was not great with regard to same sex friends, physical contact with the opposite sex was reported more than twice as often by Americans.

The picture that emerges from a comparison of these profiles is one of a culture whose members are fairly accessible to each other physically, and one whose members have only tenuous physical ties. This conclusion seems to hold true for all areas of the body, target persons, and both sexes. The contrast between the cultures is less true with regard to mothers and same sex friends, but even here the differences are substantial; they appear less striking only when compared with the relative physical isolation of the Japanese from other intimate acquaintances.

Intimacy and Isolation: Extreme Cases

The patterns of physical communication reported by the Japanese and American respondents are summarized diagrammatically in Figure 14. The drawings demonstrate the quite considerable contrast between touching patterns in the two cultures. Visual comparisons can be easily made concerning the extent of physical accessibility with each target person within each culture, and between the same target persons in the opposite culture. Again it is notable that nonverbal contact is greater with the least attractive associate among Americans than it is with the most attractive associate among the Japanese.

Some reference to individual cases may help to impart some sense of the significance of these figures. The most striking cases of limited contact can be found among the Japanese. Among the 120 persons who comprised this sample were several dozen who indicated limited closeness with acquaintances of any kind. Among these a considerable number reported *no physical contact at all* with either one parent or with the same or opposite sex friend. Though the majority of these could remember no physical contact with their fathers, several reported they had never touched or been touched by either parent. Although most reported some physical communication with friends, there were instances of nearly total isolation even from peers.

After nearly every administration of the Nonverbal Inventory to Japanese subjects, one or more students asked to speak to the investigator privately. In each instance it concerned their "shock" upon filling out the forms. It was the first time that they had

Figure 14 Physical Contact

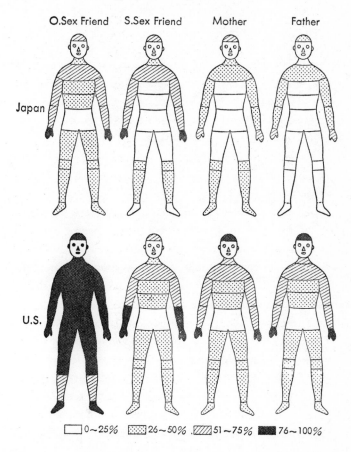

O.Sex Friend S.Sex Friend Mother Father

Japan

U.S.

☐ 0~25% ▦ 26~50% ▨ 51~75% ■ 76~100%

realized the extent of their physical isolation; some could not remember ever touching or being touched by one or both of their parents.

Among American students there were no instances of this sort of isolation. All reported physical contact with one or both parents, and friends of one or both sexes. There were instances of relative isolation, of course, but none approaching the extremes found among Japanese respondents. The extreme cases for Americans fell in the opposite direction, though extreme is scarcely a suitable word for describing a majority of a sample. Most of the students reported physical contact with an opposite sex friend in all areas of the body. Many Americans also indicated physical contact in 15 out of 24 areas of the body with even a same sex friend, and as high as 15 out of 24 areas with mothers and/or fathers.

Commentary

There is strong evidence here of cultures enforcing norms that regulate the extent and character of physical accessibility in interpersonal relationships. Although nearly every imaginable pattern of touching behavior can be found in the results, both the consistencies and the contrasts are considerable.

Much as the two cultures share the same verbal priorities, they share also an agreement concerning what is appropriate to touch and not to touch in interpersonal encounters. Neither society appears to distinguish between "touching" and "being touched," both appear to increase or decrease together. Differences between males and females, too, seem inconsequential in both societies.

Physical contact with peers is greater than contact with parents in both Japan and the United States. However, where the Japanese report nearly equal contact with both friends, Americans favor physical contact with the opposite over same sex friends. With parents the pattern is reversed: Americans show about the same pattern of contact with either parent while Japanese differentiate more sharply between them, are physically closer to their mothers and more isolated from their fathers.

The sharpest contrast concerns the general level of physical disclosure. Among Americans communication through physical contact is much more common. This holds for all potential partners. Americans are more physically accessible to mothers, to fathers, to same sex friends, to opposite sex friends. The cultural contrasts are most striking with regard to opposite sex friends with whom the Americans are much closer physically, and with regard to fathers with whom the Japanese maintain very limited physical contact.

Thus the intense physical intimacy that characterizes infancy in both cultures takes a different course through childhood and adolescence. In the United States people remain physically expressive, and touching continues to be an important channel for revealing attitudes. In Japan physical intimacy apparently decreases sharply after childhood, reducing reliance upon touch as a means of expressing inner feeling. Paradoxically the culture that creates the closest tactile communication during infancy, then, is the one that later restricts this avenue of expression; the culture that employs tactile communication relatively less during infancy later encourages use of this channel of expression.

What is the significance of the greater physical accessibility of Americans and the more limited physical accessibility of the Japanese? The findings appear to be consistent with existing stereotypes of both cultures and with the profiles reported earlier. Many observers have noted the serious composure, lack of facial expression, and gestural restraint of the Japanese. Physical intimacies are avoided and even reinforcing gestures rarely accompany remarks.

In contrast Americans are known for their physical animation, facial expressiveness, and gestural flamboyance. They rely heavily on "body English." Although the two cultures do not constitute opposite extemes in physical accessibility, they do reveal considerable contrast in their attitudes toward this channel and form of communication.

Two quite opposing interpretations might be made of this contrast in communicative styles: perhaps the atrophying of this channel is evidence of "growing up," of passing through no more than an infantile nonverbal stage on the way to communicative maturity through words; or it may represent the curtailing of an indispensable avenue of communication that hampers expression and discourages intimacy.

Infant needs are not necessarily adult needs. Nor are habitual responses to these needs carried unaltered into adult life. The newborn child passes through a series of developmental stages and in each of them certain behaviors disappear either because they no longer satisfy emerging drives or because they are replaced by more complex forms of expression. If infants have greater needs for security, for nurturance, for protection, for comfort, adults may be more strongly driven by needs for identity, for achievement, for social acceptance, or for prestige.

Adults are more than simply large infants; the limited perceptions and limited means of expression of the child are replaced by wider perceptions and more subtle means of communicating. Most important, symbols begin to mediate experience. Words provide a far more elaborate and sensitive instrument for interpreting and interacting with the world. If crying and kicking and thumbsucking gradually disappear, touch may also lose its preeminent position as a way of relating to others. The reliance upon nonverbal forms of communication, when more flexible means are available, may reflect developmental reversion to an earlier stage, or a case of retarded development. And, in many cultures, people do regard excessive and extravagant physical behavior in interpersonal encounters as "childish" or "immature." If this set of assumptions is correct then the absence of physical contact, in a person or a culture, is less a sign of inhibition than it is evidence of growth toward other forms of expression.

Yet it does not seem unreasonable to apply the same rationale to nonverbal accessibility that applies to verbal accessibility. Underlying every communicative effort is a self that in some degree seeks to be known. Every code, verbal and nonverbal, extends the resources through which the human being can accomplish this end.

Touch is, without much doubt, one of the most potent channels for the transmission of meaning. Without it, feelings of warmth, concern, intimacy and love are difficult to convey in their fullest sense. Even attitudes of frustration, irritation, and anger seem to require some nonverbal manifestation. Cutting off so fundamental a channel for the transmission of inner meaning seems as tragic in its consequences as abridgement or destruction of a sensory channel through which the outer world can be experienced.

After an exhaustive review of the scientific literature on the role of touch, Montagu concludes that rediscovery and reevaluation of its importance is long overdue. Tactile contact in infancy is essential for full intellectual, emotional and even physical development; in adult life it appears to remain of primary importance as an avenue of emotional expression. People out of touch with their bodies are often out of touch with reality and with their companions. And those who lack contact seem to suffer from their isolation. A number of disturbances, from digestive disorders to emotional illness, have been linked to some inhibition of physical expression.

On the positive side touch would seem to provide an especially sensitive way of sharing inner feelings more directly than through the medium of words. "Without tactile communication," according to Lawrence Frank, "interpersonal relations would be bare and largely meaningless, with a minimum of affective coloring or emotional provocation."[6] Even our metaphors reveal an unconscious preoccupation with this form of communication: we commonly speak of "getting in touch" and of "staying in touch" with each other. If there are meanings that can only be conveyed through words, there may also be meanings that can only be conveyed through touch. If the fullest realization of human potentials is the business of cultures, it would seem that enlarging the avenues of personal expression rather than restricting them would be encouraged.

But physical acts, because their meanings are more difficult to disguise, may be inherently more dangerous and more revealing forms of symbolization than words. A "guarded self" might be expected to minimize occasions for such communication in order to prevent overexposure of inner states. And an "expressive self" might be expected to create or welcome wider opportunities for intimate contact.

There is some evidence, though impressionistic, that limited physical expression among the Japanese is more a result of inhibition than of spontaneous choice. There are two notable circumstances in which Japanese drastically change their communicative manner. And both increase rather than reduce physical and verbal disclosure. The first is an assignment to live in a more demonstrative culture. The second is to come under the influence of alcohol. Someone once coined a term, "alcommunication," to identify the dramatic change in communicative behavior that occurs under intoxication. Both experiences seem to relax normal restrictions on disclosure. In these instances the Japanese are often as expressive and demonstrative as their counterparts in other cultures.

Clearly the sources and implications of these contrasting cultural styles require further study. But the patterns of touching reported here extend support for the assumption of a difference in motive and manner of communication in the two cultures. Not only verbally, but physically as well, the Japanese appear to reveal less of themselves, manifesting a more limited "public self," while Americans appear to reveal more of themselves physically, manifesting a larger "public self."

6 | Defense Against Disclosure of Self

All human beings, regardless of race or sex or culture, are engaged continuously in making some sort of sense of their experience. The world itself simply exists; it is without significance until given it. Neither object nor symbol contains its own meaning. If a swastika arouses feelings of religious reverence, of tribal identification, of anti-Semitism, or of political embarrassment, these derive not from the emblem itself, but from the associations attributed to it by its interpreters. That this single sign can evoke such diverse responses from a Buddhist, a Navaho, a Jew and a German should surprise no one.

To think at all, or to act at all, events must be made comprehensible. And to become comprehensible they must be placed within some system of assumptions, some framework of values, some set of intentions. Order must be imposed on confusion; coherence must overcome irrelevance; predictability must replace randomness. This conversion of chaos into cosmos is a preoccupation of human beings at every moment.

As the newborn infant matures he must form some picture of the world he inhabits and his place in it. Generally social orientations of trust or suspicion, affection or hostility, self assertion or self denial are acquired, often at considerable pain, through interactions with the environment and others. Certain objects, certain people, certain acts come to be valued—to be sought or avoided—while others lose whatever importance they may once have had. Gradually each person authors the premises on which future opinions and actions rest.

This inner cognitive world is largely unconscious, the product of a series of collisions between personal impulse and the responses favored by a particular culture. Yet this personal cosmos—which earlier we called the assumptive world of the individual—is the most precious possession we acquire. Without it, survival is impossible. Life would be absurd. There would be no way of interpreting events, and thought or action would be inconceivable.

Although the members of any culture often adopt similar ways of interpreting the world, every human being occupies a world that is in some respects unique. And it is the distinctiveness of these private worlds that makes communication between them imperative. If everyone witnessed the same events and saw them precisely in the same way conversation would be superfluous. Talking is a way of confronting differences—differences in facts, in feelings, in opinions, in behavior.

The reasons for this should be readily apparent. Every individual sees only a part of what is there to be seen. Worker and supervisor, patient and doctor, native and foreigner necessarily view the same event from different perspectives and with different purposes. Each, at best, can obtain only a fractional view of the totality of any situation. In addition, every perception is fallible. The nervous system is quite capable of error, shocking and almost unbelievable error. Sharing private perceptions with one another appears to afford the only means by which human beings can construct a more complete picture out of their separate visions and correct the distortions that confound efforts to perceive the real world. Communication also provides, of course, the conditions that stimulate human creativity for out of the expression of differences new thoughts and new possibilities are born.[1]

We would expect, then, that people everywhere would eagerly seek to disclose and share any differences in their experience. The advantages seem so obvious. But the opposite is more often the case. An undercurrent of tension arises whenever sensitive topics are to be discussed. Opposing points of view generate resistance; even discrepant facts may produce embarrassment. Human encounters often seem to generate more hostility than harmony. And the wider the discrepancies in viewpoint, the stronger the reluctance to reveal and to explore them. Why is this so?

It is, perhaps, because communication implies change. Aside from common social rituals, people nearly always converse in a context of change. What motivates people to talk is the desire to have someone see their facts, share their feelings, agree with their decisions, endorse their actions. Communication is often initiated, consciously or unconsciously, to change the other person in some respect.[2]

And, for most people, change is threatening. The deeper the change required, the stronger the reluctance to confront it. The premises which people require to make sense of their experience in the world are too vital to their sanity. And they are often, at the same time, too obscure and too precarious to withstand constant exposure to the dissonant experience of others. Agreement is sought, consistency welcomed, similarity valued. The strange, the unexpected, the inconsistent arouse alarm.

Hesitancy or retreat in the face of challenge to our private view of the world is understandable. To grant validity to the meanings of others may make our own untenable. And to change involves heavy responsibilities. It means to surrender cherished values. It requires the creation of new values. It carries an obligation to adopt ways of behaving that are consistent with the new perspective.

The sources of interpersonal challenge can easily be identified. Some people are threatened merely by the presence of those who differ from them in power, beauty, intelligence, nationality, age or sex appeal. Others are upset not by the persons with whom they talk but by the ideas they espouse. The presentation of discrepant facts, incompatible arguments, unacceptable conclusions may reveal the inadequacy of their own beliefs. Even the manner in which ideas are presented may arouse anxiety as it does when people attempt to manipulate or coerce others into accepting their point of view.

When threatened, people resort to every conceivable technique to protect their personal interpretations of events. Some retreat into silence, reply ambiguously, smile or laugh, change the subject, refuse to answer. Others resort to defending themselves by argument, rely on humor or sarcasm, rationalize their position, or counterattack. Through all these forms of defense there runs a common theme, an effort to protect the psychic self from meanings that endanger the status, the sanity, or the security of the threatened person.

In short, it appears that people desire to share their experience yet equally fear the consequences of doing so. When interpersonal threat is perceived how will Japanese and Americans respond? Do these two cultures train their members to react similarly or differently to communicative challenges? As already noted, in Japan there is an emphasis on ritualized encounters, on minimal verbal and physical disclosure. The "public self" appears to be limited; the "private self" encompasses a larger part of the personality. In the United States there is an emphasis on spontaneous self expression, upon maximum disclosure of the self. The "public self" appears to occupy a larger, the "private self" a smaller area of the personality.

Given these differences one might expect the two cultures to adopt distinctive reactions to threat. There is good reason to believe that all communicative behavior derives from a dominant inter-personal orientation. For the Japanese a desire to limit disclosure of the private self constitutes such a theme. To be consistent with this theme their style of defense against threat should be pre-dominantly passive. That is, they should prefer to avoid further exposure of their thoughts, to reduce the intensity of personal involvement and, if possible, to withdraw from further exploration of sensitive matters.

Americans, in the face of interpersonal threat, should similarly be predisposed to adopt patterns of defense that are consistent with their dominant interpersonal orientation. For them such a theme is found in their desire to express and share a larger proportion of their inner experience. Consistent with this theme is a defense of the self that is predominantly active. Again, although there may be individual variation in the specific content of their reactions to threat, the underlying intent will be similar. They will react to the perception of threat by elaborating their views, increasing their degree of involvement, and opposing those who challenge core values.

Defensive Strategy Scale

Exploratory investigation in Japan and the United States suggested a number of dimensions that should be incorporated in any instrument designed to identify forms of defensive behavior. First, the instrument should differentiate between levels of threat, permitting responses to reflect the intensity of perceived threat. It should specify—especially in cross-cultural studies—the wide range of persons who can provoke threat, and should reveal differences in the defensive tactics employed with each of them. And, of course, it should provide an opportunity to select from a spectrum of different kinds of defensive messages.

Accordingly, a Defensive Strategy Scale was developed with these criteria in mind. The instructions which accompanied this scale specify two levels of interpersonal challenge:

> In converastions we sometimes find ourselves threatened by something the other person says or asks. His or her remark brings up topics we would rather not discuss or feel uncomfortable discussing. Two levels of such threat might be described:
>
> (1) Low Level Threat: This occurs when a statement by a particular person introduces a topic or opens an area of conversation that makes you feel slightly uncomfortable. (It might refer to your political or religious opinions, matters of health, or attitudes toward work. Or it may suggest mild disagreement with your beliefs or disapproval of your actions.) Such comments make you feel *somewhat uneasy*, but they do not strongly upset you.
>
> (2) High Level Threat: This occurs when a statement by a particular person introduces a topic or opens an area of conversation that makes you feel very anxious, tense, or angry. (It might refer to your sexual attitudes or behavior, blame or guilt for past actions, or criticize you for certain failings. Or it might convey a strong disagreement with your beliefs or strong disapproval of your actions.) Such comments are *very disturbing* to you emotionally.

Earlier research also suggested that Japanese reactions to threat might vary depending on the persons who were the sources of threat. Attributes such as age, sex, status, power, and respect might be critical in determining the precise response considered appropriate or possible. Accordingly, thirteen different target figures were included on the scale: persons who are older and younger, superior and subordinate, same and opposite sex, admired and not admired, mother and father, closest same sex and opposite sex friend, and a stranger.

The scale identified a variety of defensive messages from which respondents could choose their own pattern of response. Although it was impossible, for practical reasons, to provide an unlimited list of such messages, fourteen frequently reported reactions to threat were included. The range of defensive reactions included the following: (1) Remain silent, (2) Act as if I didn't hear it, (3) Show nonverbally that I preferred not to answer, (4) Hint verbally I preferred not to answer, (5) Laugh, (6) Change the subject, (7) Reply in abstract or ambiguous language, (8) Ask others what they think, (9) Say I did not want to discuss it, (10) Try to talk my way out of the situation, (11) Answer the remark directly, even though uncomfortable, (12) Defend myself by explanation and argument, (13) Use humor or sarcasm to put them in their place, (14) Tell them to mind their own business.

In each case the respondents were asked to indicate the precise form of defensive reaction they had chosen within a specific interpersonal context. A specific defensive reaction had to be selected for each target person under conditions of low and high levels of threat. Individuals were urged not to speculate about what they *might do*, but report what they *had done* in such encounters in the past. They were reminded that there are no right or wrong answers to such questions, only honest or dishonest ones. All questionnaires, as noted earlier, were completed anonymously and without restrictions on time.

It can be seen that these defensive messages cover a wide spectrum from silence to denunciation. Yet it is possible to differentiate broadly between active-aggressing and passive-withdrawing forms of interpersonal defense. In the former the communicant handles anxiety by letting it out rather than containing it. He expresses himself more fully, extends and elaborates his position, risks deeper involvement with others, and may even counterattack those who threaten him. In the latter the communicant prefers withdrawing from further interaction. He seeks to reduce his psychological stake in the conversation, disguises or conceals his anxiety, and avoids further exposure of inner feelings on this topic or with this person.

The defensive messages described on the Defensive Strategy Scale, therefore, can be clustered according to the dominant motive and probable outcome. The first five reactions appear likely to permit one to retreat from further revelation of the self; the last five reactions would be difficult to use without becoming more deeply involved verbally and emotionally. Further disclosure of the self would be almost unavoidable.

The responses that fall in the middle of the spectrum might also be divided in this way, but their consequences cannot be so reliably predicted. "Changing the subject" and "Replying in ambiguous language" appear to be evasive maneuvers, but since they require further participation might also be seen as somewhat active forms of defense. "Asking others what they think" and "Saying I did not want to discuss it" appear to belong under the active defense pattern, but could also serve to conceal or circumvent dangerous material. Hence the focus here is on cultural differences with regard to the modes that can most sharply be identified as active or passive, the five at the opposite extremes of this continuum.

The Defensive Strategy Scale thus permits people to report their favored forms of defense against a variety of persons and under conditions of both low and high levels of threat. The results permit comparisons between Japanese and Americans, between males and females, between conversations that arouse low and high degrees of anxiety.

Cultural Differences

What forms of defense against disclosure are most often and least often reported by Japanese and Americans? When considerations of sex, of status of the target person, and of the intensity of threat are set aside, the Japanese showed a somewhat greater variety of defensive reactions. They did not rely so heavily upon one or two responses to threat; the contrast between the most favored and least favored replies was less striking.

When confronted by threatening questions or remarks, the most popular responses among Japanese were to "Say I did not want to discuss it," "Hint verbally I preferred not to answer it," and "Remain silent." They seldom chose to "Tell them to mind their own business," "Use humor or sarcasm to put them in their place," or "Defend myself by explanation or argument." With only one exception, thus, the most preferred reaction of the Japanese is "passive," and without exception the most avoided reaction was of the "active" type.

When the intensity of interpersonal threat is considered, the pattern changed somewhat. Under low levels of anxiety, when the person was slightly uncomfortable, the Japanese substituted "Answer the remark directly even though uncomfortable" for "Remain silent." They avoided replying aggressively with "Tell them to mind their own business" or "Defend myself by explanation and argument," and with the passive reaction, "Act as if I didn't hear it."

As the intensity of the threat increases Japanese relied more upon "Say I did not want to discuss it" and the passive forms, "Remain silent" and "Hint verbally I preferred not to discuss it." Under high threat conditions they rarely chose to "Defend myself by explanation and argument," "Tell them to mind their own business," and "Answer the remark directly, even though uncomfortable." Thus, with only a few exceptions and regardless of the level of anxiety, the Japanese appeared to prefer withdrawal to aggression in the face of threat.

A rather different profile emerged from the replies of Americans to the same interpersonal circumstances. When considerations of sex, of status of the target persons, and intensity of threat are set aside, Americans showed a sharp rather than a slight difference between the defensive forms they favored and rejected. The two most frequently reported responses, for example, were chosen more often than all other available responses combined. The overwhelming reaction to threat was to employ such active forms as "Answer the question directly, even though uncomfortable" and "Defend myself by explanation and argument." The replies least employed in response to threat were all at the passive end of the scale where Americans rarely reported using "Ask others what they think," "Laugh," and "Change the subject." The preference for active forms of defense was striking with all five of the most chosen responses falling at the aggressive end of the scale.

Even varying the degree of threat did not change the defensive style of Americans. With only a slight shift in the order of ranking, they continued to prefer active responses to threat no matter whether it was of a low or high level of intensity. And the least favored reactions to threatening remarks continued to be passive or ambiguous in form.

Sex Differences

Are there differences in the way males and females respond to threatening interpersonal situations? One might expect so. But the results do not support a sex difference in defenses. Partly this may be due to cultural distinctions overriding sexual ones. Americans distinguished so sharply between preferred and avoided responses to threat that their scores offset the more subtle differences found among the Japanese. But the expectation of a large sex difference in defensive styles may be incorrect. To be born Japanese or American appears to be far more influential in determining styles of communicating interpersonally than being born male or female.

When male and female patterns are examined within each cuture some sex differences appeared. Yet the contrasts were less dramatic than anticipated. Japanese males and females preferred the same, predominantly passive, reactions to threat: "Say I did not want to discuss it," "Hint verbally I preferred not to discuss it" and "Remain silent." Both sexes in Japan also avoided active defenses, rejecting "Tell them to mind their own business" and "Defend myself through explanation and argument." Males avoided "Try to talk my way out of the situation" while females avoided "Use humor or sarcasm to put them in their place."

Japanese males and females also favored similar defenses with both levels of threat. Under low anxiety both preferred to "Answer the question directly, even though uncomfortable," "Hint verbally I did not want to discuss it," and "Say I did not want to discuss it." As anxiety increases "Answer the quesion directly" was dropped and the more passive "Remain silent" was substituted. The defensive responses avoided by both sexes differed slightly, but not markedly. Under low threat males and females rarely "Tell them to mind their own business" or "Use humor or sarcasm to put them in their place." Under higher threat the same active defenses were rejected although males also avoided "Ask others what they think" and females avoided "Defend myself through explanation and argument."

Among Americans, males and females also showed considerable consistency in their reactions to threatening interpersonal situations. Males and females both preferred to meet all types of threat by choosing an active response: "Answer the question directly, even though uncomfortable," "Defend myself by explanation and argument," and "Use humor or sarcasm to put them in their place." Both also rejected the same forms of defense, that is, "Ask others what they think," "Change the subject," and the passive reactions, "Laugh" and "Act as if I didn't hear it."

Again, when various intensities of threat are compared, both sexes in the United States overwhelmingly adopted the same active tactics: "Answer the question directly, even though uncomfortable," "Defend myself by explanation and argument," and "Tell them to mind their own business." Rejected patterns of defense were also nearly identical under both levels of threat, both avoiding "Ask others what they think," "Change the subject," and the passive responses, "Laugh" and "Act as if I didn't hear it."

Throughout the data on defensive communication there is substantial, though not complete, support for the conclusion that the Japanese culture discourages the use of "active" forms of response and encourages "passive" patterns of defense. The evidence on the former is stronger than on the latter. Also, it appears that Japanese draw upon a wider repertoire of defensive responses, and do not concentrate so exclusively upon those categorized as passive. Still, a majority of their choices are of the passive, or self-inhibiting, type. And they consistently reject the more active ways of replying to interpersonal challenge.

In contrast, the communicative style of Americans demonstrates a clear preference for "active," or self-assertive, reactions to threatening remarks. There is no instance, regardless of the intensity of threat or the sex of the respondents, when further explanation and argument, is not the most popular reaction to the threatening behavior of others. Passive responses are consistently among the least chosen, or most rejected, forms of defense.

Adaptation to Target Persons

Do the defensive postures of Japanese and Americans change with different communicative partners? Again one would expect so. And expect that the Japanese, living in a vertically organized society, would be far more sensitive to differences in age, rank, power, sex and prestige than the Americans. But the data did not confirm this expectation, or confirmed it less strongly than anticipated. While Japanese did manifest a wider diversity of defensive reactions, they showed only slight adaptation to the status of their communicative partners.

There were some tendencies toward distinctive reactions to the source of interpersonal threat: with older and superior people the Japanese reported more often they preferred to "Remain silent," "Hint verbally that I preferred not to discuss it," and "Reply in abstract and ambiguous language"; with younger and subordinate persons they retained the latter two but substituted as their preferred response "Say I did not want to discuss it." With people they particularly respect Japanese chose most often to "Remain silent" or "Answer the question directly," but with those they do not respect they chose to "Remain silent" or "Say I did not want to discuss it." Mothers or fathers who arouse anxiety were handled with identical reactions: "Say I did not want to discuss it," "Answer the question directly" or "Remain silent." The same defenses were favored with opposite and same sex friends except that remaining silent dropped out as a popular reaction.

As noted earlier, the Americans made a much sharper distinction between the defenses they favored and those they rejected. The most frequently chosen reply was selected two or even three times as often as the most popular reply of the Japanese. Further, there was a striking consistency in defensive response that cut across all categories of communicative partners. That is to say the same defensive reaction was employed with nearly everyone regardless of status, sex, power, or relationship. Most Americans, most of the time, preferred to "Answer the question directly, even though uncomfortable" or "Defend myself through explanation and argument." In all but two instances these were by far the most common reactions to threat, and the two exceptions involved persons who were younger or who were not respected. Even here Americans preferred an active response: "Tell them to mind their own business" and "Use humor or sarcasm to put them in their place." Americans, it seems, were far more consistent in defensive behavior, while Japanese employed a wider number of responses to threat and were somewhat more discriminating about the target person with whom they were employed.

The general pattern of preference for active or passive responses to social threat are in the predicted direction in these two cultures. But the lack of a stronger and more consistent adaptation to status among the Japanese is somewhat surprising. It may be that between eighteen and twenty-four years of age people have a stronger need to resist the threats posed by others as a way of maintaining an uncertain identity. It may be that members of this age group, particularly in Japan, are not yet fully aware of the significance their culture attaches to such distinctions in status. Or, it may be that the findings are evidence of a culture in transition, that Japanese society is, in fact, shifting from its traditional vertical orientation to a more horizontal or egalitarian structure.

Individual Patterns of Defense

Emphasis upon the most preferred and most rejected modes of defense may oversimplify the findings. There was considerable variation in individual profiles. People manifested many different strategies in reaction to invasions of the private self. This variability was less marked among Americans, but it appeared in both samples to some extent.

In threatening interpersonal settings some people relied heavily upon only one or two defensive tactics. In the case of the Japanese it was usually a preference for remaining silent, laughing, or replying ambiguously; in the case of the Americans it consisted of talking their way out of a situation or defending themselves through argument.

Yet some respondents employed a broader range of reactions to anxiety arousing encounters: where certain subjects differentiated little between low or high degrees of threat, others employed almost a totally different repertoire of defenses if they were mildly or seriously upset. If some discriminated little among threatening associates, relying upon a single form of reply, others showed immense variability, using a distinctive defense for almost every target person.

Commentary

There are cultural factors that complicate the interpretation of these findings. Threat is usually a product of perceived differences in meaning and intent. Yet the value attached to such differences, and particularly to the verbalization of them, may not be the same for both cultures. As recently observed, "Americanism rises on foundations of ultimate dissent: Japan, on foundations of ultimate assent."[3] If this is true, and there is good reason for believing it is, the two cultures may view conflict in distinctive ways.

It can be assumed that the more topics people talk about, and the more completely they discuss them, the more they will experience conflict. The Americans, as a consequence of their greater desire to articulate their ideas publicly, should encounter disputes more often. The Japanese, because of their lower communicative profile—the more limited scope of their conversations and the containment of inner thoughts—should encounter conflict less often. Yet the intensity of threat that is experienced, as compared with its frequency of occurrence, may operate in reverse. Vulnerability seems to be a function of concealment: the intensity of anxiety aroused by any expression of difference depends on the extent to which the self is hidden or manipulated. In this respect the findings suggest that while greater censorship of the self may reduce the probability of confrontation, it may also intensify the depth of threat that is experienced whenever conflicts do occur.

Even the conception of communication itself—its proper function and intended outcome—appears to differ in the two cultures. For the Japanese, conversation is a way of creating and reinforcing the emotional ties that bind people together. Interpersonal attitudes are its content. Intuition is its mode. Social harmony is its aim. The pursuit of truth is less critical than the maintenance of rapport. Or, put another way, subjective feelings are valued above objective facts. Differences of opinion, and particularly arguments, since they may disrupt the atmosphere and divide the group, arouse apprehension. As one student remarked, "I dread open conflict more than anything." Another noted, "Even among friends I find it difficult to discuss one's thought or feeling unless we are already convinced we agree." Both commented on the impossibility of reestablishing a normal relationship after having had an argument with someone. As Halloran suggests, confrontation or *tairitsu*, must be avoided at all costs.[4] If not, someone will have to surrender or be defeated, someone will be embarrassed and lose face, someone will be hurt. No one wants to be placed in that position, nor wants to put anyone else in that position.

The view of communication that prevails among Americans stands in some contrast to this. Interaction provides an opportunity for the expression of personal meanings, hence becomes an arena for confrontation. Ideas are its subject matter. Argument is its means. Valid conclusions are its aim. The maintenance of rapport is less important than stimulating a variety of points of view. (Opposition is thought so critical to establishing the truth that the "devil's advocate" has been created to counteract occasional instances of too much harmony and unanimity.) The success of conversation is often measured by the excitement generated through a clash of opposing points of view and the number of insights arising from the argument. Participants in discussion are chosen to guarantee a diversity of perspectives; debates are encouraged as a productive way of exploring and resolving issues. Clashes of opinion, unless highly personalized, do not usually alienate friends; they may even be welcomed as a way of deepening relationships.

Such distinctive views of the social function of communication may account, at least in part, for some of the contrast in defensive styles. The Japanese, fearful of the divisive potential of outright clashes of opinion, appear to be among the most diligent of peoples in preventing such clashes from occurring. Conflict tends to be intercepted before it can be expressed; disagreement is often muted to reduce its impact. Formalizing human relationships is one way of limiting the extent of differences that may be sanctioned. Ritualizing interaction so that conversations conform to social expectations rather than personal impulse tempers frankness of expression. One Japanese described his communication as a three-act play: "Premeditation," "Rehearsal," and "Performance." Each encounter is planned in advance, messages rehearsed, and remarks offered according to plan. The aim is to anticipate disagreements and avoid any challenges that could embarrass or harm others. Since outright clashes are less likely to occur and are less brazenly expressed it may be less important for Japanese to develop active forms of defense against them.

The opposite would seem to be the case among Americans. Although seldom as spontaneous or authentic as claimed, these qualities are sought and respected in relations with others. Free speech is more than a political ideal, it is an interpersonal one as well. Genuine dialogue is the aim, confrontation is permitted. Interpersonal rituals, since they postpone a meeting of minds or disguise the nature of differences, arouse impatience. Any constraints upon saying what one thinks or feels seem incompatible with personal honesty or valid group conclusions. Having encouraged the expression of individual differences, Americans must develop an ability to explore and resolve the resulting disagreements. Where one culture arranges social encounters so that outright disputes rarely occur or are reduced in intensity, the other admits such differences and must then cultivate active responses to the threat they pose.

Language, the primary instrument of communication, appears to reinforce these cultural attitudes. The concept of cultural relativity—that every society manifests a somewhat unique system of values and these support a particular social order and manner of behavior—is paralleled by the concept of linguistic relativity. This idea, first articulated by Benjamin Lee Whorf and Edward Sapir, holds that human beings do not inhabit an objective world, each person seeing only what is there to be seen and interpreting it in similar ways, but that users of every symbol system are, in part, prisoners of the language they employ. Every medium, paradoxically, bestows both opportunity and limitation upon its user. One cannot convey the same truth through a piece of music, a mathematical formula, or a painting. Nor does a pencil, piece of charcoal, or paintbrush inspire identical interpretations of a scene by an artist. Similarly, language is not a mirror of reality as commonly supposed, but is itself a shaper of reality. What is experienced must be grasped and articulated according to the categories available in a particular tongue. Events must be ordered so that they conform to the rules of a particular grammar. To be intelligible at all, every remark must reflect the assumptions and the logic implicit in the syntax of the language of a specific culture.

The two languages that are involved here appear to differ sufficiently in vocabulary and grammar to compound the analysis of defensive behavior. Not only are certain concepts that are present in one language lacking in the other, but there are more profound differences that could affect the incidence of conflict and the character of defenses against it. Japanese is a more ambiguous and more evocative language than English. Sentences are not as closed with respect to meanings, encouraging listeners to consider a multiplicity of interpretations. There is less precise identification of referents. Article, number and gender are not specified. The representation of time is less complex. The subject of a sentence is often unstated, carried by implication rather than explication. A sentence fragment or phrase will often suggest rather than describe an event. As Maraini notes in speaking of the Japanese language, "It does not tend to clarity, to accurate definitions of when and where and exactly how many people and of what sex are doing this, that, or the other. Instead, it prefers to suggest, leaving the details vague, surrounding the subject with approximations rather than revealing or disclosing it."[5]

Ambiguity, of course, cuts two ways. It makes the assertion of any opinion more dangerous since the speaker has less control over the meaning assigned to it; a mild criticism that is phrased ambiguously may be interpreted as a sharp rebuke. Yet it also provides a better vehicle for passive defense, permitting the speaker to obscure a vital disagreement in an equivocal statement; a vague remark provides a form of reply without really saying anything.

The two languages, hence, may predispose their users to communicate in ways that capitalize upon rather than run against the potentials they possess. Both are capable of a vast range of subtle discriminations. But where English seems more sensitive to discriminations among ideas and objects, Japanese seems more sensitive to discriminations among persons and their social relationships. The unique properties of these two languages thus may affect the frequency, form and resolution of disputes.

It is not merely the medium of language that governs communication, but the patterns of actual usage within a culture. Even if all meanings could be expressed in all languages, cultures would still create unique norms for human encounters. As noted earlier, the Japanese seem more skeptical of the power of words. It is felt that spoken utterances can never really do justice to inner thoughts. Reality appears too diverse, too complex, too changeable to be captured in a skein of words. For this reason the Japanese are mistrustful of bold assertions, and less optimistic about argument as an avenue to truth. As Inazo Nitobe has written, "To give in so many articulate words one's innermost thoughts and feelings is taken as an unmistakable sign that they are neither profound nor very sincere."[6] Americans, on the other hand, seem to admire explicit verbalization of issues, seem confident that through sincere and persistent efforts problems can be articulated and solved. To many Americans, Japanese avoidance of a prompt and explicit reply to any inquiry is patently indirect and evasive; to many

Japanese, the glib and candid response of Americans is equally insincere and unconvincing. If the American cannot understand why he gets such puzzling answers to such simple questions, the Japanese cannot understand how anyone can give such simple answers to such puzzling questions.

Conversational etiquette, too, reveals sharp differences in priorities. A member of Japanese society is always surrounded by superiors and subordinates, and the presence of either modifies the way he must phrase his views. At the outset, the relative status of each communicant must be known. An exchange of *meishi* (personal identity cards indicating name, organizational affiliation, and position) is no mere formality, it is essential in fixing the appropriate mode of address. The choice of words, the selection of prefixes, the proper form of verbs turns on the status and respect accorded the listener. The greater the emphasis upon the vertical ranking of people, especially when such distinctions permeate every remark, the greater the potential for threatening contacts. Among Americans, introductions are cursory, disregarded, or even dropped. Not only are differences in status less marked and less emphasized, but they have less bearing on the form and content of remarks. Conversations often run their course with no apparent recognition of, or adaptation to, such differences.

The reticent and modest style of Japanese speech also stands in contrast to the vigorous and unrestrained style of Americans. Japanese appear reluctant to call attention to themselves, prefer to minimize claims to expertise, and usually understate the views they assert. Quiet remarks, hedged in qualifications, gain credibility because of the cautious and tentative way they are offered. If, as Maurice Bairy notes, Japanese society rewards those who "stand in," American society appears to reward those who "stand out."[7] Exaggeration is the most noted (and criticized) feature of American speech. If Americans are hungry, they are "starving"; if they are thirsty, they are "dying for a drink"; if they are cold, they are "freezing to death"; if they are warm, they are "cooking." Contemporary appeals to "tell it like it is" seem to demand even more exaggerated expression of personal attitudes. It is as if only extreme and profane language will make a personal opinion credible. Such contrast in habits of language usage undoubtedly multiplies the incidence and heightens the intensity of intercultural misunderstandings.

Communication in Western cultures can be described as predominantly discursive and dialectic in form. It consists of exploring issues by alternately posing and answering a sequence of questions. The outcome depends on the relevance and clarity of the questions, and upon the accuracy and completeness of the answers. The pattern appears in classrooms, courts of law, parliamentary bodies, deliberative committees, in ordinary conversations. But it is not the dominant mode in Japan. Here direct questions are often regarded as a breach of manners. Outsiders teaching in Japan find that raising questions in classrooms fails to stimulate discussion; shoppers find a direct inquiry concerning a price may only elicit comments about the size or color of the article; personal questions elicit replies that convey only that the remark was heard, understood, appreciated, but provide no opening for further exploration or disagreement. Noncommittal phrases such as *"ma, so desu"* not only supply little in the way of information, they tend to block further conversation in that vein.

Outright questions, if they must be asked at all, are phrased so they can be answered in the affirmative rather than the negative. This, of course, often requires that the speaker know the answer before putting his question. Not only are direct questions avoided, but assertions, too, are made less contentious in tone through sentence endings. The ubiquitous *"ne"* which transforms declarative statements into questions seeks to elicit continual agreement from the listener. Conversation proceeds not by negation, as it does in the West, but by affirmation. Talk serves to identify areas of consensus rather than areas of conflict. Conversations based on assertion and counterassertion differ in content and especially in atmosphere from those that are based on a sensitive and persistent search for agreement.

If the Japanese tend to avoid direct questions, they tend no less to avoid direct answers. This is especially the case if the answer is "No." It is one of the few Japanese words which, after it has been learned, is avoided in actual conversation. "No," as someone said, is automatically an offensive and insulting expression. Several studies elaborate this feature of Japanese speech. Keiko Ueda found the Japanese employing sixteen different ways of avoiding the necessity of saying "No."[8] Another study, focusing on the expression of negative feelings, concurs with this conclusion. Silence, avoidance of eye contact, indirect and ambiguous replies were all used to avoid expressing outright disagreement; even positive feelings, such as liking and loving, tended to be conveyed by the eyes, tone of voice, silence, or by actions, rather than by words.[9] Unqualified assertions are seldom made unless the speaker is sure others will agree with it. "When faced with no alternative but to disagree," Richie writes, the Japanese "will construct a context such that no is the only answer that can satisfy all his restrictions. But he will avoid direct contradiction."[10] This is obviously not a limitation inherent in language. Japanese contains as wide a vocabulary of negative words as any language. It is, instead, a matter of usage. And in this regard there may be few cultures which so restrict the use of such a basic term.

Many of the distinctive norms of the two societies regarding conflict are manifest in the process of decision-making. In the United States problems are sharply defined, causes of difficulty identified, alternative proposals offered and challenged, decisions hammered out through a process of argument and compromise. In Japan, decision-making follows a different course. The discussion may proceed at some length without any clear specification of the problem. Participants proceed cautiously, attempting to decipher the opinions of others without asking them directly. Various points of view are intimated, but so expressed that they can later be qualified or retracted if they encounter resistance. The leader in the American case alternatively challenges and crystallizes the views expressed. He presses to effect a decision in the allotted time. In the Japanese case the leader sensitively listens for or nourishes whatever themes seem to be drawing unanimous support. At any suggestion of a serious difference of opinion the meeting may be postponed. Perhaps at another time group members may be more of the same mind. If not, the matter can and should be delayed until everyone is comfortable with its disposition. Differences appear to be emphasized and encouraged in the United States as a way of stimulating a wider variety of solutions. Differences appear to be minimized or suppressed in Japan in the interest of preserving the harmony of the group.

Although all these factors complicate the study of defenses, they help to explain rather than contradict the findings. Evidence of a cultural contrast in defensive behavior remains. And it appears consistent with the boundaries on the public and private self favored by these two societies. Americans, it seems, not only express themselves more fully, but prefer defenses that are also more active and self-assertive. And they prefer this pattern regardless of the intensity of threat or the status of the source. They choose to defend themselves through verbal explanation and argument and, if forced to, through denunciation and counterattack. All are active responses, all are highly involving, and all lead toward greater instead of lesser disclosure of the self.

Among the Japanese the range of response is more varied.

There is less concentration upon one or two modes of defense. Consistent with more limited disclosure, Japanese seem to prefer more passive reactions to threat. They choose to remain silent, hint verbally or hint nonverbally that the topic is inappropriate or unattractive. Rejected modes of defense more sharply reveal this difference in communicative style; Americans consistently avoid passive responses to threatening situations, and Japanese almost equally avoid the more active forms of defense.

Other cultural norms support and encourage this difference in defensive style: in one society the emphasis is upon preserving harmony, upon preventing confrontation, upon respecting status differences, upon modest and qualified assertions, upon avoiding direct questions and frank answers, upon preventing divisive or alienating compromise; in the other the emphasis is upon self assertion and confrontation, upon equality of status, upon vigorous and authentic assertion, upon blunt questions and candid answers, upon critical examination of personal views, upon adjudication and integration of differences. Societies, like organisms, cultivate consistency and coherence, and this seems as true of communicative styles as of any other cultural features.

7 | Reflections

Cultural parochialism seems an outdated and potentially disastrous base on which to build life in a global village. Along with the divine right of kings and manifest destiny, ethnocentrism belongs among the relics of belief once held viable but no longer relevant to human survival. Technical advances alone—satellites, jet aircraft, ballistic missiles—remind us that a global village is more a hard reality than a poetic metaphor.

Before we can create the family of man required to inhabit such a global village, much remains to be done. Cultural parochialism flourishes and has always flourished on cultural isolation, so that wider and more frequent opportunities for interaction among the peoples of the world is essential. Yet interaction alone, as we are reminded daily, carries with it no guarantee of mutual respect. Familiarity, it is said, breeds contempt. At least it does when contact consists only of uncomprehending confrontation. People have always been frightened or antagonized by those who see the world very differently or who communicate their intentions in bizarre ways. The record of the past consists largely of a tiresome repetition of the same script, one whose principal theme has been the eradication of diversity. The more nations perceived themselves to be alike in important respects the more amicable their relations; the more they perceived themselves to be different—in faith, social custom, political belief—the more they sought to destroy each other.

More than mere contact is essential. People must become capable of empathy, of being able to project themselves into the assumptive world, the cultural unconscious, of an alien culture. Yet that is a formidable task unless there are ways to introduce people to the assumptive world of others. "One of the handicaps of the twentieth century," writes Ruth Benedict, "is that we still have the vaguest and most biased notions, not only of what makes Japan a nation of Japanese but of what makes the United States a nation of Americans, France a nation of Frenchmen, and Russia a nation of Russians. Lacking this knowledge, each country misunderstands the other."[1]

It is this handicap that prompted the present investigation of cultural differences. If intercultural rapport requires some grasp of the way others see the world, the way they interpret their experience, and the way they express themselves, it seems reasonable to assume that insight into communicative styles might be prerequisite to appreciating other kinds of differences. As Edward Hall once put it, "Interaction is the hub of the universe and everything grows from it."[2]

In carrying out this purpose two cultures, Japan and the United States, have been examined with regard to their patterns of communication. Not only have their broad features been identified, but the content of verbal, nonverbal and defensive messages has been studied in detail. At this point the separate findings can be brought together, the consistencies and contrasts noted, and the personal and social implications explored. However, there are cautions that should be observed, especially in assaying anything as complex as the communicative style of a culture. One impulse to resist is claiming or implying that in proving something one has explained everything. Another danger is that of oversimplifying; it is satisfying to capture some aspect of human behavior in a credible formula, but it can be misleading if it obscures the variability in its operation in specific circumstances. There is also the risk of overconfidence; we are often better at believing than we are at seeing. Partially confirmed hypotheses come to be viewed as closed matters and discourage further exploration.

Yet some facts are better than none, qualified conclusions better than no conclusions, and partial explanations superior to none at all. The search for useful knowledge stops only if the partial and tentative are treated as comprehensive and absolute. It is wise to remember that the value of any inquiry into human conduct lies not only in the conclusions to which it points but in the further questions it raises.

Public and Private Self: Revisited

To Bashō's question—"My neighbor, how does he live?"—we can now venture some partial and tentative answers. At the outset a basic proposition was formulated to guide inquiry into the communicative manner of Japanese and Americans. It was this: the proportion of the self that is shared with others, the public self, and that which is not shared with others, the private self, differs in these two countries. The Japanese, it was predicted, would prefer social encounters in which the extent of thought and feeling shared with others was relatively small, while the proportion not disclosed was relatively large. The opposite was predicted for Americans: they would conduct conversations so as to maximize the expression of thought and feeling and to minimize the portion of the self that was not disclosed. This contrast in communicative intention, it was predicted, would lead to differences in verbal and nonverbal expression within each culture and would complicate efforts to achieve understanding between the two cultures.

The first hypothesis derived from this proposition was that the Japanese would prefer to communicate more selectively with predictable associates while Americans would interact more freely and with less discrimination. Although not tested directly, there is indirect support for this conclusion. Americans, it was found, disclosed more of themselves to strangers than the Japanese, communicated more consistently verbally and nonverbally with all associates, and relied on the same defensive approach regardless of the personal characteristics of the threatening persons. In contrast, the Japanese were less disclosing to all target persons including strangers, and were more discriminating in their disclosures and defenses with people of varying status.

It was predicted that the Japanese would prefer more regulated and Americans more spontaneous forms of communication. Encounters that conform to social conventions require only stock messages and stereotyped replies, thereby reducing personal involvement and limiting disclosure of the private self. Spontaneous forms of communication, due to their less predictable course and content, provide opportunity and necessity for fuller personal expression. Here, too, the evidence is suggestive rather than definitive. The cultural profiles were highly distinctive. The Japanese described themselves and were described as "formal," "reserved," "cautious," "evasive," and "silent." It would be difficult to imagine a set of attributes more consistent with a preference for ritualized interaction. Americans described themselves and were described as "frank," "self assertive," "spontaneous," "informal," and "talkative." Again it would be hard to construct a profile of traits more compatible with a preference for spontaneous conversation. Most interesting, the profiles were nearly complete opposites. Communicative traits assigned to Japanese were almost never assigned to Americans; those features most often attributed to Americans were rarely attributed to Japanese. The cultural profiles lend support to the notion that the two cultures have different conceptions of the ends of communication and promote distinctive ways of realizing these ends.

To test the accuracy of these abstractions the content of ordinary conversation was examined in the two cultures. The first analysis focused on the topics talked about, the persons with whom they were discussed, and the level of disclosure in face-to-face communication. In Japan and the United States there was surprising agreement on what people liked to talk about and what they did not like to talk about. Matters of taste, attitudes toward work, and opinions on public issues were reported to be most thoroughly discussed, while financial matters, personal traits, and physical attributes were less deeply explored in both countries. A similar hierarchy also existed with regard to conversational partners. Japanese and Americans were both most open with peers, next with parents, and least with strangers. Where the Japanese were more discriminating in disclosure to same or opposite sex friends and to mothers and fathers, Americans tended to differentiate little in what they revealed to peers or parents. The sharpest cultural discrepancy concerned fathers: among Japanese they were markedly less attractive as communicative partners, but among Americans fathers were nearly as attractive as mothers.

With regard to the level of conversation, however, the cultures differed sharply. Japanese rarely reported talking in more than "general terms" on any topic to any person. Americans, on the other hand, disclosed on all topics to all persons at deeper levels and often approached "full and complete detail." The contrast was consistent across topics and target persons: on the most sensitive topics (physical and sexual attributes) Americans disclosed more completely than the Japanese did on all but the least sensitive topics (taste in food, television programs); with no partner did the disclosure of Japanese approach the level of Americans with all intimate acquaintances. On the average, Japanese communication with fathers only slightly exceeded the depth of communication Americans reported with strangers whom they would never meet again.

Examination of individual cases confirmed this cultural assessment. Some Japanese revealed almost nothing about themselves on any topic to any person; many more reported they did not disclose themselves deeply to anyone. Replies to a questionnaire, "What I am like in interpersonal relationships," echoed this same theme: Japanese reported they shunned strangers, felt uncomfortable with acquaintances, avoided expressing inner feelings, guarded against any impulsive acts, withheld contradictory opinions, maintained a calm and cool facade. When asked, "What I wish I were like in interpersonal relationships," they reported wishing they could be less tense, less frightened, more open, more courageous about their ideas, more honest, reveal more of what they felt they were really like. "The Japanese," says Ichiro Kawasaki, "veils himself in an atmosphere of secrecy, even when there is nothing to hide."[3]

In short, the findings support the hypothesis that the Japanese communicate significantly less of their inner feelings and thoughts even with their most intimate acquaintances. Americans, in contrast, appear to express themselves across a wider variety of topics at a significantly deeper and more personal level. Verbally the public and private selves of Japanese and Americans differ.

It was also predicted that nonverbally, through the avenue of physical contact, the Japanese would be less accessible than Americans. The findings supported hypothesized patterns. Again the cultures demonstrated similarities as well as differences. Both societies agreed on areas of the body that can and cannot be touched: the areas of greatest contact included the hands, shoulders, forehead, back of neck, head, and forearm; the most rarely touched areas were the front and rear pelvic regions, thigh, and lower leg. There was general agreement, too, on who would and would not be touched: the greatest contact reported by Japanese was with their opposite sex friend, mother, same sex friend, and father in that order; Americans reported nearly the same pattern except for reversing the rank of same sex friend and mother. Where Japanese displayed nearly the same degree of physical communication with opposite and same sex friends, Americans showed much greater contact with opposite sex friends; where Japanese differentiated sharply between parental figures, reporting considerably greater contact with mothers than with fathers, Americans appeared to be as close physically to their fathers as their mothers.

While both cultures endorsed a similar ranking of areas of contact and of persons who could be touched, the extent of contact revealed a dramatic difference. Touch as a form of interpersonal communication, was indicated nearly twice as often in all categories by Americans as by Japanese. Americans indicated nearly twice as much contact with mothers and three times as much contact with their fathers as did the Japanese. Although the amount of physical communication with same sex friends was nearly alike in both cultures, contact with opposite sex friends among Americans was more than double that reported by Japanese.

The cultural profiles drawn from these findings are clearly distinctive. In one, people are relatively isolated, have only tenuous physical ties to one another, are less expressive and accessible physically, are apparently discouraged from using this channel to convey inner states or attitudes. In the other, people are closer,

145

have more frequent physical contact, are more expressive and accessible, and rely more heavily upon this channel for conveying inner feelings. Individual cases again point up this cultural contrast. Some Japanese reported almost no contact with either parent, and a number recalled never touching or being touched by their fathers. Although most Japanese reported some physical contact with peers, there were instances of very limited contact with opposite or same sex friends. In no case did any American approach this degree of physical isolation. Extremes among Americans fell at the opposite end of the spectrum. Here, instead, were instances of great physical closeness with both parents, and total contact with opposite sex friends. The evidence with regard to physical communication in the two cultures seems clear: in Japan physical expression and intimacy are discouraged, limiting the extent to which the self is revealed nonverbally, while in the United States physical expression and intimacy are encouraged. Thus the patterns with regard to both physical and verbal disclosure are consistent with predicted cultural differences.

Another way of testing any speculation is to explore it under extreme conditions. If, as the evidence so far indicates, there are cultural differences in communicative styles, how do the two cultures handle stressful conversations? It was hypothesized that the Japanese, in keeping with their more guarded view of the self, would prefer to reduce involvement, and prevent further disclosure under conditions of threat. Americans, in keeping with their more expressive style, might prefer defensive reactions that would necessitate further disclosure. In short, the former should prefer passive forms of defense (flight), the latter should prefer active forms (fight).

Scores obtained from the Defensive Strategy Scale supported some of the predicted contrasts. The clearest pattern was manifest by Americans. Their dominant response to threatening remarks, regardless of the intensity or source, was to "Answer the remark, even though uncomfortable," "Defend myself through explanation and argument," "Use humor or sarcasm to put them in their place," and "Tell them to mind their own business." The first two, by far the most highly chosen, are active forms of defense while the latter are aggressive or even hostile in tone. Americans favored further disclosure no matter who was the source of threat or whether it was slightly or very disturbing. They rejected defenses that involved flight or a passive reaction.

Japanese defensive behavior was more complex, but not inconsistent with predictions. Japanese employed a wider variety of defenses. They preferred most to "Say I did not want to discuss it," "Hint I preferred not to dicuss it," "Remain silent." Only under low levels of threat did they choose to "Answer the question directly, even though uncomfortable." The Japanese were also somewhat more discriminating in their responses to the source of threatening remarks. Disturbing comments from older and superior persons were answered differently than those from younger or subordinate ones; reactions to threats originating with respected or unrespected persons also differed somewhat. Thus there is strong if not conclusive evidence of cultural divergence in coping with anxiety-arousing interpersonal encounters, and it tends to confirm the different communicative orientations of the two cultures. The Japanese consistently avoided active and aggressive tactics in favor of more passive ones that reduced opportunity for further disclosure. Americans consistently reversed this pattern and prefer the very tactics the Japanese renounced.

There is more than a suggestion here of cultural circularity, the cultivation of one communicative norm forcing the cultivation of a compensating one. A society that encourages wider and deeper expression of personal meaning exposes its members to more frequent and wider differences of opinion. This increases the extent of threat and forces people to develop the poise and tactics to resolve such arguments productively. Another society which limits the depth of expression reduces the incidence of threatening confrontations and has less need of such direct ways of handling conflicts. If this is true, and there is reason to believe it is, one culture copes with differences by ritualizing encounters to avoid outright clashes while the other is forced to cultivate active ways of coping with unavoidable conflicts of opinion.

Finally it was suggested that the extent to which the inner self is disclosed affects the accuracy with which the self is perceived. Can anyone know another person unless that person becomes accessible through some form of communication? Can anyone even know themselves until they can observe their own acts and words? If this is true, then the more completely the self can be expressed, the more it is available to be known by self or other. Unfortunately, this is a more elusive and complex hypothesis to test. The data reported here support a difference in the extent to which the self is disclosed verbally and nonverbally in Japan and the United States, but the figures do not provide any estimate of the accuracy of perceptions of self or others. Some suggestive data is reported in the work of Abate and Berrien who found Americans to have a somewhat more accurate perceptions of themselves than did Japanese.[4] More complete evaluation of this hypothesis will have to await further refinement in measuring instruments.

Psychic Implications

Having gone this far in identifying two cultural styles of communicating, we now seek the significance of these findings. In what ways do these cultural patterns restrict or enlarge human potentials? In what ways do they diminish or enrich human relationships? Toward what social pathologies do they tend if carried to extremes?

Any such speculations are obviously hazardous and controversial: hazardous because they require projections beyond the immediate data, and controversial because they implicate the values of each interpreter. Yet to evade such issues seems nothing more than a common form of intellectual cowardice. Merely to gather facts without reflecting on their meaning seems neither intelligent or useful. The form and content of our communication with others is a matter of personal choice, but for people to disregard the consequences of their own style of interacting neither frees them from such consequences nor permits them to choose other ways of interacting. It seems better, therefore, to attempt some appraisal of these cultural styles even if such appraisals are fallible, than to refuse to acknowledge the impact of such differences on the individual, the group, and society as a whole.

What are some of the psychic consequences of the distinctive communicative norms these cultures promote? Does discouraging expression of thoughts and feelings reduce opportunities to actualize the self? Will inhibiting inner impulses drive them irretrievably into the unconscious? Does the withholding of feeling reduce the capacity for feeling? Or, conversely, does giving wider and fuller expression of inner states help people to more fully realize their own potentials? Will encouragement for offering ideas in turn stimulate having more ideas? Does sharing feelings enlarge the capacity for rapport?

This idea can be put more boldly still: Is expression of the self essential to growth of the self? The impulse to symbolize, to transform raw experience into significant form, appears wired into the human nervous system. It is, after all, the differentiating feature of the species. It is as natural to symbolize—through music or drawing or speech—as it is to breathe. The newborn infant and mature adult clearly differ in the richness, subtlety, depth, and complexity of their reactions to life for the human personality is formed through experience, and the wider and deeper the experience the better. Deprive a child of musical instruments or of drawing materials and you limit growth in each of these areas. Isolate a child or refuse to interact with him and it will almost certainly reduce his capacity for sensitive and productive relations with other people. Mental retardation is often less a matter of inheritance than of growing up in an environment that discourages self expression.

Capacity for healthy human relationships seems to expand with opportunity for interaction. As Goffman has written, "There seems to be no agent more effective than another human being in bringing a world for oneself alive, or, by a glance, a gesture, or a remark, shrivelling up the reality in which one is lodged."[5] The ability to expose one's self, to be known to at least some other person, argues Jourard, is a prerequisite for a mature and productive personality.[6] Research on the process of therapy reinforces this view. It is apparently the challenge of deep verbal involvement with another human being that is critical in aiding recovery and promoting growth.[7]

Unusually gifted and creative people—artists, poets, playwrights, scientists—appear to experience both inner and outer worlds more abundantly at least partly because of a drive to articulate their insights. To many, like Picasso, the inducement for creative work arises from the social environment: "To fall back, to live on oneself, to withdraw is sterility. Communication with the exterior means fertility."[8] Or, as the critic Harold Rosenberg once put it, "in order to get any truth about myself, I must have contact with another person." The opportunity to express opinions is very often the stimulus for having an opinion. Even the proverbial man on the street is often astonished at the depth of insight he displays when asked to voice his ideas. Encouragement of fuller communication would seem to encourage growth. The unused, unexpressed self atrophies.

To this charge that restrictions on self expression limit human potential the Eastern cultures take some exception. Is not silence as essential as speech in the cultivation of personality? Must sensations always be articulated for them to acquire significance, or can people achieve deeper and more personal meanings through introspection? If inhibition contributes to psychic impoverishment, can not excessive disclosure also cripple? The self, it is argued, grows not through noisy argument but through quiet contemplation. All conversations need not take place out loud or in the company of others; internal conversation can be as penetrating and stimulating as external conversation. Meditation and contemplation are respected not because they imprison the mind, but because they free it. (It is paradoxical, perhaps, that respect for this sort of interior dialogue now enjoys growing favor and respect among the same Western cultures that oppose any restriction on uninhibited expression.)

The glorification of verbalization and encouragement of greater private disclosure may end by being *self* defeating. "Speech," writes Kiyoshi Ikeda, "draws everything out of a man, and when words have been spoken there is nothing left in him."[9] If many Westerners in Japan are sometimes annoyed by Japanese reluctance to express themselves more directly and completely, there may be as many who, after returning to their own cultures, are embarrassed at the extent of overintellectualization and oververbalization they now notice at home.

Is there sufficient inner experience to justify such great disclosure? Those who continually give out, who can always provide some statement, can have little energy left for taking in, for noticing or assimilating the world outside themselves. A compulsion to express seems at least as great an impediment to true selfhood as cultural norms that inhibit such disclosure. It is more important to have something to say than to have to say something.

The totally revealed person, the one whose public and private self are the same, may lose rather than gain a sense of who he is. A self that encloses nothing, may be nothing. As Georg Simmel suggested many years ago, the boundaries of the private self may not be breached without diminishing the ego that remains.[10] The Japanese artist—actor, writer, dancer—and ordinary person as well may resist the temptation to express everything that can be expressed for this not only leaves the sender depleted, but deprives the receiver of all creative opportunity as well. People who reveal themselves totally leave nothing further to be discovered. As such they become bores. The irrepressible self may be as questionable an ideal as the overly contained self.

In assessing the current wave of Western enthusiasm for group encounters which promote private disclosure, George Steiner questions the values of such extended confessional experiences: "What's the point of self discovery if there's nothing to discover? Having (people) go even deeper inside themselves only shows them what bores they are. It would be better if they would memorize poetry, or learn a language, or play chess, or listen to music, or study butterflies."[11] Repression may at one time have thwarted self realization; today a sense of inner emptiness may result in part from such encouraged transparency.

The extent of self disclosure undoubtedly results in part from differences in child rearing habits in the two countries. An American infant is surrounded from birth by an appreciative audience that rarely interrupts efforts to provoke some sort of communicative expression from the infant. To hold the attention of this audience and to secure its approval, children learn to speak often, loudly, and dramatically (as any performer does). In adulthood it would not be surprising if this tendency toward verbalization and exaggeration should continue as a primary means of securing recognition and love. Japanese children appear to be loved no less, but are seldom subjected to such constant stimulation from adults. Words are less important; being together in silence is quite enough. Thus in adulthood communicative styles in the two cultures may carry a different psychological significance. Among Americans expressive efforts may arise from greater emphasis on self realization or may reflect a continual craving for constant attention and affection. Among Japanese the reduced drive for expression may indicate repression of natural impulses or simply a lack of need for such constant stimulation or reassurance.

Differences in child rearing practices may give rise to a difference in communicative focus as well. In one culture communication is turned principally outward. It is an opportunity for creative expression, for self actualization, for achievement. It is a means of using inner resources to influence and affect the outer world. In the other the process of communication is turned more inward. It is less a means of individual performance or for exerting influence and more a way of achieving inner serenity and harmonious relations with society. The pursuit of change, inside or outside the self, is less compelling. Such a contrast in communicative thrust would understandably affect the character of conversation in the two nations.

Even the concept of the self cannot be taken for granted as consistent from one culture to another. Physical identity and psychological identity do not always coincide. Every society creates some entity or unit that serves as a psychological center of the universe for its members, the ultimate source of meaning and the locus for the interpretation of events. In some it is the individual. In others it is the work group. In still others it is the extended family (sometimes including even ancestors). It is this psychic unit that mediates all experience, that provides the incentive and frame for all behavior. Perhaps in no society is the private self altogether erased, but the boundary may be sufficiently elastic to incorporate others as an intrinsic part of its own identity.

In the United States, and in most Western cultures, this psychological unit is the solitary human being. The individual is the measure of all things. Identity must be claimed and defended by each person for himself. Integrity—the sense of inner harmony and wholeness—resides within the ego of each separate member of society. To preserve this sense of personal uniqueness and personal identity, the individual must often stand apart or even stand against other members of his family, office, neighborhood, or nation.

In Japan the critical psychic unit may enclose not merely the person, but all others who make up the nuclear group. It is this group that becomes the measure of all things; its identity must be asserted and defended above all. A sense of dignity and security against the hazards of life come from its strength, not from the strength of autonomous individuals. To sustain its inner harmony and wholeness people respect the needs of the group over selfish needs. Even integrity is a property of the group rather than the property of the individual. Too frequent or too strong an assertion of personal independence threatens its solidarity.

Yet some nagging doubts persist. While the individual and group need not be set against each other, their aims are often in conflict. And, because of its immense authority, the singular individual is readily sacrificed to the good of the group. There are more than a few specialists, even among the Japanese, who question whether the authority of the group has not gone too far in suppressing or subverting individual expression. One of Japan's leading psychiatrists describes at some length a common syndrome among his patients: "Many patients confessed that they were then awakened to the fact that they had not 'possessed their self,' had not previously appreciated the importance of their existence, and had been really nothing apart from their all-important desire to *amaeru*. I took this as a step toward the emergence of a new consciousness of self, inasmuch as the patient could then at least realize his previous state of 'no self.'"[12]

This pathology arises, Takeo Doi feels, as a consequence of cultural encouragement for Japanese to affiliate not as independent individuals but in a symbiotic relationship of mutual dependency. "I can say," he writes, "only that the Japanese as a whole are still searching for something, something with which they can safely identify themselves so that they can become whole, independent beings."[13] Much of the theory concerning mental illness and a great deal of experience in treatment support the idea that a dialogue with others involving disclosure of the self is an inducement to growth. "It is not until I *am* my real self and I act my real self," says Jourard, "that my real self is in a position to grow."[14]

Perhaps the two cultural perspectives help to define the pathological extremes on a continuum of disclosure. An extensive review of research on this subject suggests as much: both the person who rarely discloses himself and the person who is preoccupied with disclosure appear maladjusted and unable to maintain close relationships.[15] Private reflection and public disclosure, thus, combine in a communicatively mature person. Here there is a capacity for private contemplation that is neither a product of repression nor a defensive retreat and a capacity for public disclosure that is neither an aggressive exploitation nor a compulsive drive for attention.

Communicative Implications

Specialists in the field of communication are understandably fond of repeating that in human affairs "misunderstanding is the rule and understanding the happy accident." There is every reason to respect this assessment, for interpersonal understanding is often difficult to achieve. Every person inhabits a world of his own, and every experience acquires a singular meaning. Carried to an extreme this condition condemns people to totally alien worlds, each imprisoned in meanings of his own that are unintelligible to his neighbors.

Each society counteracts this fateful tendency toward communicative anarchy by creating a universe of discourse for its members. It invents a language, or a spectrum of languages, by which people can similarly name events and seek a common terminology for bridging their differences. Through such codes people are able to overcome some of the isolation built into human existence.

Yet impediments remain. The central issue is to what extent the communicative norms of cultures aggravate or counteract these inherent obstacles to human understanding. Japan with its emphasis on formalizing relationships reduces the scope of verbal disclosure, limits physical intimacy, and encourages withdrawal from threatening confrontations. The United States encourages more informality, permits greater verbal candor and physical expressiveness, and favors more aggressive solutions to threatening encounters.

The extent of interpersonal isolation in the two cultures was not an issue in this study. But there is some evidence that it may be greater in Japan than in the United States. Americans not only report deeper relationships with parents and friends, but their accessibility to strangers is somewhat greater. Few Japanese enter easily or often into conversations with unknown people; among Americans such behavior is commonplace. Japanese appear to prefer close ties to a limited number of friends and relatives, and indifference toward people outside this sharply bounded group. Yet the ties to intimate acquaintances, long lasting as they often are, do not seem to be very deep. Thus one culture seems to favor human relations that are intensive and extensive, and the other endorses a more limited communication with a smaller circle of acquaintances.

The depth of reported conversations leads to the feeling that human contact is somewhat superficial in both societies. Even with the most intimate acquaintances, large areas of thought and feeling remain unexplored and unshared. As Robert Oppenheimer once said, "it is as if we had neither the time nor skill nor desire to tell each other what we have learned nor to listen nor to welcome the enrichment of our common understanding." Human beings appear to spend much of their lives trying to overcome a sense of alienation while studiously avoiding their closest allies—other people—in this struggle.

Every culture, of course, cultivates some formality, some distance, some dishonesty in human relationships. The question, as Sidney Poitier once phrased it, is how far we encourage these tendencies: "We are all lonely at times, fearful at others, and pained most of the time. Why we do not make use of such kinship rather than ignoring it, is a question worth answering." If cultures could be placed along a "disclosure gradient" neither Japan nor the United States would occupy the extreme ends. But there would be a wide gap separating them. In Japan people rarely discuss in more than a superficial way any subject beyond their taste in food, television programs, films, music or reading. This, apparently, is the deepest communication they experience with anyone in their lives, even those closest to them. Among Americans there is deeper disclosure on a wider range of topics. There are many instances of talking in full and complete detail in areas of taste, work, public issues. Even in more inaccessible areas of experience there is at least a modest sharing of self.

In infancy there is no private or public self, there is only a single, undivided self. When joy is experienced it is announced; when pain is known it is expressed. Yet societies oppose this "childish" impulse to say what one thinks and share what one feels, and by adulthood an inner split is accomplished and the self is compartmentalized. But this division, necessary or not, is bought at a price. It takes immense psychic energy to monitor inner reactions continuously, carefully segregating what can be revealed from what must be concealed. This inner guardedness makes it difficult for people to "let go," to experience events deeply, makes them ultimately suspicious and afraid of their own impulses. They must continually stand guard over their own lives, sensitively weighing public reaction to every word and gesture. The results may not merely alienate people from each other but from themselves as well. While all societies erect some boundaries between what people may think and what they may say, there is reason to question how extensively this repression can be practiced without damaging the personality. It would be surprising if such concealment, practiced over a lifetime, would not limit the depth of personal sensitivity as well as the capacity for intimate relationships.

Equally serious is the way in which such interior manipulation of the self corrupts communication. Even when people earnestly and honestly seek to understand each other there are difficulties that arise from the nature of human experience and from the means of transmitting it that make such an achievement doubtful. Every person occupies a world of his own. No two people perceive alike or believe alike. Each brings to every conversation a different history, different assumptions, different motives, different expectations. Even the words and gestures they rely on to bridge this experiential divide are vague and diverse in meaning.

But these intrinsic difficulties are compounded through the addition of another factor: conversational partners often do not allow themselves to be known as they really are. Each presents, in part at least, a facade; what is felt is hidden, what is believed is falsified. The messages that ordinarily might be taken as clues to inner meaning are now deliberately managed to camouflage that meaning. If communication is difficult when people express themselves authentically, imagine the complications when each presents a person who is not really there. As Jourard points out, "When we are not truly known by the other people in our lives, we are misunderstood."[16] Concealment does not merely complicate understanding, it *encourages misunderstanding*. If one succeeds in comprehending another human being, it is only a contrived, public image that is known, not the real or private self. Two public selves interact while two private selves remain strangers. Many of the people who complain so bitterly over difficulties of communication are the same ones who inhibit or manipulate every spontaneous impulse in the maintenance of a particular image or facade. The realization of a role is sought over the realization of a unique self. Whatever potential existed for interpersonal encounter has atrophied through the repeated substitution of deceit for authenticity.

If people share little of themselves, even in their most intimate relations, what precisely is the meaning of friendship in the two cultures? One European observer of Japanese society suggests "There is no friendship in the sense that we know it in Europe."[17] Friendships are often accidents of birth and of occupation, less often of free choice. Marriage, the most intimate of all human associations, is more often arranged than spontaneous. Interaction is ritualized even among friends, and seemingly provides less of the challenge that might contribute to growth in either person or in the relationship itself. "We sometimes talk about our troubles when we meet," writes one student, "but we talk about them very generally and never go very deep. There ought to be thousands of occasions and thousands of persons with whom we could speak about such things."

In the United States friendships, though extremely transient, rarely lasting more than a few months or years, appear to involve people more deeply while they last. To some this might indicate that more ritualization is needed to preserve longer relationships. But the "Kleenex friendships" of Americans seem to follow more from extreme mobility and fluctuating interests than from internal dissension. One of the features of such friendships may be a higher frequency of conflict. This sort of interpersonal turbulence seems to be viewed by Americans with a mixture of resignation and excitement: resignation because it seems an inescapable consequence of two unique people struggling to share their lives deeply, and excitement because it provides both with an opportunity to know themselves better and to reach new depths in their relationship through the new facets that such confrontations reveal.

In still another way cultures may affect the course and quality of communication. Successful interaction involves not only encoding or symbolizing of inner states, but decoding and comprehending such symbolization. The communicative consequences of cultural emphasis upon "talkativeness" and "self assertion" among Americans may cultivate a highly self-oriented person, one who prizes and expresses every inner response no matter how trivial or fleeting. The communicative consequences of cultural encouragement of "reserve" and "caution" among Japanese may produce an other-oriented person, who is highly sensitive and receptive to meanings in others. As a reserved Japanese pointedly reminded a talkative American who had criticized his quietness, "I want to understand this other person and the only way I can put myself in his shoes is to empathize with him. And that is impossible if I am always shouting at him." Some cultural differences, therefore, may encourage a sort of communicative specialization (and communicative negligence). What one society does well another may do poorly. Yet ability to articulate *and* to comprehend are essential to any search for mutual understanding.

Social Implications

If one were forced to choose only a few words to capture the ethos of these two societies they might be these: Homogeneity, Hierarchy, Collectivity, and Harmony for Japan; Heterogeneity, Equality, Individualism, and Change for the United States. Each of these concepts seems at the same time to be a source and a consequence of the communicative styles fostered in each culture.

Is there any large country that can surpass Japan in the homogeneity of its people? As a nation it has deliberately cultivated "Japaneseness" for hundreds of years, consciously isolating itself from foreign influences and promoting the greatest possible consistency in values, language, architecture, clothing, rituals, and life styles. The more any two people communicate, the larger their store of common meanings and the more they come to resemble each other in outlook. And the more two people resemble each other, the easier it is to convey complex meanings through the simplest and most rudimentary messages. Husbands and wives, for example, often exchange a volume of meaning with a single word, a glance, a gesture. And convey it with great accuracy. If this is true of any interpersonal relationship then the fragmentary and ambiguous character of Japanese communication so often cited by observers may be simply a projection on a national scale of the same phenomenon found in ordinary dyadic interaction. The greater the cultural homogeneity, the greater the meaning conveyed in a single word, the more that can be implied rather than stated.

In Japan nearly all interaction takes place within an elaborate and vertically oriented social structure. Every person has a distinct position and status within this framework. Rarely do people converse without knowing, or determining at the outset, who is above them and who is below them. (A factor that contributes, possibly, to reluctance to talk with strangers.) Associates are always older or younger, debtor or creditor, male or female, subordinate or superior, younger sister or older sister. And these distinctions all carry implications for the manner of approach, form of personal address, choice of words, physical distance and demeanor. As a result, conversation tends to be ritualized, reflecting the formal hierarchy of relationships. This, too, may make statements that seem vague to outsiders capable of carrying quite precise meanings. It has, however, two further effects: it moderates the articulation of different points of view and, at the same time, increases preoccupation with losing or saving face.

As noted earlier, group identification is paramount in Japan. The boundaries of the ego appear weaker and more permeable than those that surround the collective unit. A "limited social nexus," the family and work group, provide the motive and meaning for life. "A Japanese," suggests Maraini, "does not exist; he is a cog in a social mechanism."[18] Though overstated, the Japanese does tend to be more other-directed than self-directed, more dependent than independent, more conscious of social responsibility than of responsibility to self. His orientation is collective rather than individual. It is the group that should grow, prosper, survive, and it is the group from which the individual obtains support, identity, and pride. Much of his communicative behavior, therefore, is focused not on securing attention or advantage for himself, but to sacrificing self to secure advantage and prestige for the group.

The aim of communication is to extend control over physical and social events, and to enlarge and enrich the experiencing of these events. To achieve these ends is a delicate matter when it requires the blending of private impulses in collective units and when everyone occupies a distinctive position in a complex hierarchy. To preserve harmonious relations becomes the overriding concern in interpersonal encounters. Each person must be sensitive to the status of others and to the possibility that some thoughtless remark may weaken or dissolve the group. It is as if interaction took place between people balancing on a plate whirling in space. They move around it gingerly lest a misstep or unexpected maneuver upset the equilibrium and cast them into a psychological void. To protect the plate and to keep the balance is paramount. Great social sensitivity and elaborate social rules give some protection against the destructive potential of unanticipated and uncongenial remarks. A concern for others and loyalty to the group are valued above concern for self and private integrity; courtesy and tact are prized above honesty and sincerity.

Standing in sharp contrast to the homogeneity of Japanese culture is the heterogeneity of the United States. It has been populated by waves of settlers from Northern Europe, Southern Europe, Africa, the Far East, from every continent and country of the world. Immigrants continue to arrive in diminishing though still substantial numbers. The result is a culture that is a mosaic of cultures. Differing concepts of time, of space, of art, of family life, of design, of dress, of manner continue to coexist in an uneasy truce. In large urban centers dozens of foreign newspapers flourish, "natives" often speak "foreign" tongues, a spectrum of rituals and religions are practiced, and schools often conduct classes in several languages to accomodate new arrivals. While the process of assimilation continues (as it does in every encounter), understanding cannot be taken for granted. The segregation that once reduced the frequency and ritualized the content of interaction across racial lines may be diminishing, but as it recedes it has exposed the magnitude of ethnic differences that still characterize this culture and that complicate communication within it.

In spite of such heterogeneity, or perhaps because of it, equality has been a dominant cultural theme. De Tocqueville described American commitment to it as "extreme," "incessant," "insatiable." "They will endure poverty, servitude, barbarism," he wrote, "but will not endure aristocracy."[19] The suggestion of any semblance of superiority or privilege is automatically condemned. It has been suggested that respect and deference are among the most painful emotions Americans experience. No equality, of course, is complete or permanent. But the emphasis on it as an ideal and the degree of its attainment in the United States, according to Eric Larrabee, is unequalled: "Compared to any country in Europe, for example, the United States is so lacking in traces of status as to have, in European terms, virtually no social system whatsoever."[20] In this sense, Japan resembles the nations of the world far more than does the United States. The lack of complicating status considerations may ease communication, make for greater approachability with strangers, and encourage greater consistency in verbal, nonverbal, and defensive messages.

This same equality, it is thought, contributes to the extreme individualism that is the most marked feature of the social landscape. Equality, as De Tocqueville emphasized, places people side by side, forces each to rely on his own impulses, requires each to find his own reasons. If group affiliation provides the incentive for social interaction in Japan, it is self realization that is a compelling motive in the United States. As one foreign student put it,

"America is the land of the Big I." Personal authenticity, individual fulfillment, spontaneous expression, private commitment, and personal influence are cultivated and often attained. The urge to speak out, to express personal conviction, to take a stand, to influence others is so compelling that automobile bumpers carry arguments to and from work, proclamations cover the surfaces of buildings, political posters hang from house windows, announcements overflow bulletin boards and kiosks, grafitti fill up the walls of public toilets, even lapel buttons carry opinions. It is as if there were not enough times, not enough platforms, not enough channels for personal expression. Strength in this society lies not in the capacity to surrender to the group, but in the capacity to stand alone or even against the group. Conforming, though by no means absent, is regarded as a form of psychic suicide. Integrity is a private matter; self actualization is the aim. Extensive personal disclosure, even if it involves more provoking conversations, is the course for fulfilling this aim. Having isolated each other, the art and technique of associating together and of accomodating diversity becomes imperative.

A fourth feature of the American cultural scene is its commitment to change. Historically the nation sprang from dissatisfaction with traditional institutions. The geography of the frontier supported an experimental attitude. Physical mobility, the movement across the land, and social mobility, the absence of confining status barriers, made continual adaptation a necessity. These harmonized well with other cultural features. A nation of individuals, especially one so heterogeneous in composition and so dedicated to diversity, exposes itself to continual stresses that require innovation. As a result not only the land but social relations and even personalities came to be seen as resources to be explored, cultivated, and improved. It is in this sense that the United States resembles a nation of missionaries. Everything is, and should be, made over. Interpersonal relations are not fixed for life but are transitory or, if they continue for a longer time, do so because they promote mutual growth. Friendships are to be cultivated. Personality is not fixed, but evolving; it is something to be probed, worked over, improved. In such a social system encounter is essential. The validity of change, cultural or personal, must be tested through dialogue. Discussion and debate, the most prominent communicative forms in Western cultures, involve proposals and counter proposals, assertions and refutations, leading to agreement on critical principles or actions.

One suspects that the two cultural styles differ not merely in this or that technical detail, but that they spring out of distinctive conceptions of the role of communication in human society. Even the language used to describe communication in each culture reflects this difference in outlook. In one there is continual reference to the search for harmony, the importance of form, the control of feeling, the cultivation of empathy, the sharing of mood, the observance of rituals, the search for consensus, the preservation of the whole. Discord spoils the mood; it is not in good taste. The view and vocabulary are essentially *esthetic*. Interaction is a vehicle for the attainment of inner and outer resonance. In the other there is a search for insight and truth, the cultivation of independence, the exploration of differences, the desirability of confrontation, the respect for argument, the stimulation of creative discovery, the achievement of practical conclusions through compromise. Too much unanimity means stagnation, it removes the stimulus for improvement. The view and vocabulary is, essentially, *pragmatic*. Communication is seen as an instrument of personal and social accomplishment. Both views of human interaction exist in both societies, of course, but which is dominant seems to change from one culture to the other. In Japan communication seems better suited to preserve the peace; in the United States it seems better suited to disturb the peace.

When members of the two cultures meet certain communicative difficulties can be expected. Insistence upon full disclosure, on verbal frankness, on vigorous argument may, to a Japanese, seem an abuse of privacy and a threat to continued relations. Insistence on formalities, on verbal tact, on avoidance of argument may, to an American, seem an unproductive approach and a threat to continued relations. The actions of each are, in part at least, unintelligible to the other. Faced with such incomprehensibility, each explains the other to himself by recourse to his own cultural mode and his own cultural assumptions. The Japanese seems "deceitful," "devious," "inscrutable." The American seems "arrogant," "domineering," "quarrelsome." As long as this remains the case differences are compounded by misunderstanding and even mistrust.

Extremes, of course, exist in both cultures. There are Japanese who are open, impulsive, direct, talkative. And there are Americans who are quiet, reserved, introspective. Contact at this border between the cultures demonstrates the possibilities for intercultural rapport. But there is another cultural border. This is where extremely formal and inarticulate Japanese meet face-to-face with extremely voluble and aggressive Americans. Here one can glimpse the immense challenge of intercultural communication.

Each of these cultural styles, pushed to extremes, carries its own destructive potential. If in the United States an equalitarian ethic erects few barriers to social intercourse, it fails at the same time to generate any sense of communal identity or communal obligation. This becomes more isolating still when it combines with a loud insistence upon individual autonomy and the right of everyone to act on every impulse. Worship of the self and pursuit of individual autonomy isolates the individual from the rest of the human race. As James Reston put it, Americans have "liberated themselves into loneliness."[21] Like the tenuous figures sculpted by Giacometti, each person is so preoccupied with standing alone that each lacks the means of relating to others. Over a hundred years ago De Tocqueville saw the danger in an extreme individualism: "Each of them, living apart is a stranger to the fate of all the rest... he is close to them, but he sees them not; he touches them but he feels them not; he exists but in himself and for himself alone."[22] The same warning can be found in more contemporary assessments. Slater, for example, emphasizes the myriad ways Americans try to minimize or circumvent any dependence on others, seeking not only a private house but a private office, private means of transportation, private garden, private telephone, private television. "An enormous technology," he writes, "seems to have set itself the task of making it unnecessary for one human being ever to ask anything of another in the course of going about his daily business.... We seek more and more privacy, and feel more and more alienated and lonely once we get it."[23] A young Israeli student, upon returning from a visit to the United States commented, "Here in Israel we all have the feeling that we serve some common cause, that there is some meaning for all our efforts. But there you can't find anything of this kind. Everybody is for himself."[24] Although pleasant for a short time, he felt afterward that the culture seemed empty and without significance.

A society of separate individuals, each preoccupied with his own self fulfillment, reduces to no society at all, but to anarchy. When concern for the individual is untempered by involvement with others, self assertion easily transforms into arrogance and exploitation. Perhaps it is not so surprising that a society that worships self expression is also one that ranks highest in the incidence of personal assault and violence.

There appear to be two ways of compensating for this extreme dedication to individualism. Both are currently in evidence. The first is to unite individuals legally. Lacking sufficiently strong affective ties, concern is simply legislated. Not only have written constitutions and contracts long been a ubiquitous feature of American society, but the idea of contracts has lately been extended into such intimate relationships as those between student and teacher, husband and wife, and parent and child. Even love may soon be quantified and negotiated. Perhaps, as the theologian Reinhold Niebuhr once argued, the creation of a just relationship is the first step toward community—certainly it is a protection against injustice—but it is hardly an improvement on mutual responsibility based on affection. The second way of compensating for an isolating individualism is to cultivate the art of associating and the capacity for human empathy. There is evidence that this, too, is taking place. No society in the world is supported by so extensive a network of communal organizations for pursuing common causes. The human sensitivity and encounter group movement not only originated in the United States, but has its widest and most enthusiastic support there. It may be that the aggressive friendliness and ever-present smiles, the insistence upon informality and constant use of personal pronouns, the extent of private revelation and amount of touching, may simply be symptoms of isolation and an effort to reestablish a lost sense of community. Yet the findings of this study, instead, suggest that Americans are in close communication with each other verbally and nonverbally, that they share their inner experience in considerable depth, and are capable of exposing and exploring their differences with considerable candor.

If one society seems threatened by a fanatic individualism, the other may be vulnerable to a fanatic collectivism. Where rights are emphasized in one, obligations appear to dominate the other. The individual in Japan is firmly positioned within an intricate hierarchy, albeit generally benevolent, that supports and protects, but that also predetermines the course of his life and surrounds him with a never-ending burden of responsibilities. Friendships are more often determined by birth, sex, school, and work than by simple attraction; marriages are often mechanically arranged rites of passage. Spontaneous encounters undoubtedly are more precarious, but they may also be less likely to become a burden and more likely to challenge or stimulate. Social intercourse that is highly ritualized consists mainly of programmed exchanges that discourage dialogue and supply little nourishment.

The power of the group and the importance attached to unanimity can be so great that differences are neither welcomed nor permitted. Any distinguishing feature, from a distinctive personal opinion to a distinctive style of dress, may so threaten the harmony of the group that it is a cause for ostracism or expulsion. The Japanese, as Benedict and so many others have insisted, ask too much of the individual. "They require him to conceal his emotions, to give up his desire, to stand as the exposed representative of a family, an organization, a nation."[25] Constant inhibition and constant sacrifice can end by distorting or destroying whatever is unique and precious about an individual human being.

Conformity carried to extremes ends by denying selfhood altogether: the risk in Japan is less one of alienating people from each other than of alienating people from themselves. Deference—yielding to others out of respect—easily becomes submission—yielding to others out of fear. And a submissive self is an invitation to domination; authoritarian exploitation appears the greatest risk in a self-denying society. Again, it may not be surprising that among industrialized nations Japan has the lowest incidence of criminal assault and, at the same time, the highest rate of personal suicide.

Here the bonds that hold the community together are supposedly those of affection and obligation. Yet a society that emphasizes human relationships, that stresses mutual responsibility, that cultivates intuitive listening, that values empathic understanding, should also be one in which interpersonal ties are close, deep, warm, challenging. But the findings of this study do not support such expectations. According to our data the harmony is superficial rather than deep. There is little evidence of wide social contacts, of extensive personal disclosure, of physical intimacy, of candid exchanges of ideas or creative utilization of differences. People are connected, but they rarely seem to meet.

To Americans, a Japanese might well say, "You Americans so inflate the importance of your private selves that you run the risk of destroying the bonds that hold a humane society together." To this an American might reply, "In your concern with harmony you run the risk of discouraging individual growth which is the ultimate strength of any social system." Obviously both countries have much to say to each other; both have need of teaching and learning from the other. Person and group are inalienable: No human being ever developed without the stimulation and incentive of a surrounding human community; no society can survive or grow without continual fertilization from creative individuals.

Conclusion

The suspicion is widespread that modern civilization is faltering in its efforts to hold the human community together or to realize the full potential of the individual member. Despair over the low quality of human communication is a major theme of our day. Painters portray man tortured with doubt, fragmented, alienated from others. Sculptors show the individual standing alone, immobilized and mute in an interpersonal void. Novelists from

Kafka to Abe to Camus describe a society in which people stare at one another through self-made masks, muttering slogans and cliches. On our stages the family is portrayed as a ";delicate balance," one so fragile that a single authentic feeling can destroy it. Human relations are described as object relations. The dominant philosophical chord seems to be the inability of human beings to know themselves and to let themselves be known. Rarely do people reach one another, and when they do, rarely do they have anything important to say.

It is hard to believe that our artists, playwrights, novelists, poets, and lyricists are entirely mistaken. Nevertheless, they share the view that despite our technology and affluence we have much to learn about how to relate to one another humanly. The most serious danger is that pessimism will prevail, a mood of impatience and intolerance born of an insistence upon immediate solutions will overwhelm us. "Our task," said Martin Buber, "is to get in touch." Yet to create a world in which people are in touch with each other requires a world in which people are willing to search for the truth about themselves.

There can be no inner dialogue without an outer one; no outer dialogue without an inner one. Mind and heart grow not only in social isolation but through confrontation with other minds and hearts. No person obtains much nourishment from his image in a mirror, or from someone who is only a reflection of himself. There is a communicative paradox here: The more one human being resembles another, the more pleasant and effortless their relationship tends to be, but the less they can learn from each other; the more another person differs, the more puzzling and challenging the relationship, but the more they can learn from each other. To see oneself through the eyes of a neighbor can be stimulating, but to see oneself through the eyes of a member of a foreign culture is, in truth, a "mind-blowing" experience. Not only does it free one from the prison of cultural parochialism, but introduces one to fresh ways of experiencing the world.

The boundaries of our countries are no longer the borders of our minds. It is vitally important—perhaps even a matter of survival—that we come to comprehend and appreciate what other peoples feel and know. This kind of interpersonal empathy can enlarge human perspectives and multiply opportunities for personal and cultural growth.

REFERENCES

1. Communication in a Global Village

1. Reischauer, Edwin. *Man and His Shrinking World.* Tokyo: Asahi Press, 1971, pp. 34–5.
2. Kunihiro, Masao, "U.S.–Japan Communications," in Henry Rosovsky (Ed.), *Discord in the Pacific,* Washington, D.C.: Columbia Books, 1972, p. 167.
3. For a fuller description of the process of assigning and communicating meaning, see Dean Barnlund, "A Transactional Model of Human Communication," in J. Akin and A. Goldberg (Eds.), *Language Behavior,* The Hague: Mouton, 1970.
4. Byrne, Donn, "Interpersonal Attraction and Attitude Similarity," *Journal of Abnormal and Social Psychology,* 62, 1961.
5. Triandis, Harry, "Cognitive Similarity and Communication in a Dyad," *Human Relations,* 13, 1960.
6. Runkel, P., "Cognitive Similarity in Facilitating Communication," *Sociometry,* 19, 1956.
7. Rokeach, Milton. *The Open and Closed Mind.* New York: Basic Books, 1960. (Denny has just completed his first jump to the East.)

2. Public and Private Self

1. As quoted in Liberman, Alexander. *The Artist in His Studio.* New York: Viking Press, 1960, p. 142.
2. Luft, Joseph and Harry Ingham. *The Johari Window, A Graphic Model of Interpersonal Awareness.* Los Angeles: University of California Extension Office, 1955.

3. Profiles of Two Cultures

1. The concept of *amaeru,* an important one for an understanding of Japanese interpersonal relations, has no simple English equivalent. "To presume upon another's benevolence" might have been slightly closer to its Japanese meaning, but even this falls short of capturing its full implications. See Doi, Takeo. *The Anatomy of Dependence.* Tokyo: Kodansha International, 1973.
2. Shigeta, Midori. "Ambiguity in Declining Requests and Apologizing: An Experimental Study of Japanese and American Patterns." Paper pre-

sented at the Conference on Intercultural Communication, International Christian University, 1972.

3. Richie, Donald, "The Japanese Character," *Orientations*, 1970, p. 27.

4. Benedict, Ruth. *The Chrysanthemum and the Sword*. Boston: Houghton Mifflin, 1946.

5. Halloran, Richard. *Japan: Images and Realities*. Tokyo: Tuttle, 1964, p. 226.

6. Guillain, Robert. *The Japan I Love*. New York: Tudor, n.d., pp. 11, 78.

7. Nakamura, Hajime. *Ways of Thinking of Eastern Peoples*. Honolulu: East-West Center Press, 1964.

8. Seike, Kiyoshi and Charles Terry. *Contemporary Japanese Houses*. Tokyo: Kodansha International, 1964, p. 12.

9. Nakane, Chie. *Japanese Society*. Berkeley: University of California Press, 1970, p. 35.

10. Matsumoto, Yoshiharu, "Contemporary Japan: The Individual and the Group," *Transactions of the American Philosophical Society*, 50, 1960, p. 60.

11. Abate, Mario and F. Berrien, "Validation of Stereotypes: Japanese Versus American Students," *Journal of Personality and Social Psychology*, 7, 1967.

12. Caudill, William, "Japanese American Personality and Acculturation," *Genetic Psychology Monographs*, 45, 1952.

13. Fenz, Walter and Abe Arkoff, "Comparative Need Patterns of Five Ancestry Groups in Hawaii," *Journal of Social Psychology*, 58, 1962, p. 84.

14. See Joseph, Franz (Ed.). *As Others See Us: The United States Through Foreign Eyes*. Princeton: University Press, 1959.

15. Broughton, Morris, "From South Africa," *ibid.*, p. 268.

16. De Tocqueville, Alexis. *Democracy in America*. New York: Mentor, 1965 (Original date of publication, 1835), p. 163.

17. Gorer, Geoffrey. *The Americans*. London: Cresset Press, 1948, p. 101.

18. Abate and Berrien, *op. cit.*

19. Caudill, *op. cit.*

20. Fenz and Arkoff, *op. cit.*

4. Verbal Self Disclosure

1. Jourard, Sidney. *The Transparent Self*. Princeton: Van Nostrand, 1964.

2. Jourard, Sidney and Paul Lasakow, "A Research Approach to Self Disclosure," *Journal of Abnormal and Social Psychology*, 56, 1958.

3. Guillain, *op. cit.*, p. 11.

4. Moloney, James. *Understanding the Japanese Mind*. New York: Philosophical Library, 1954, p. 126.

5. Krisher, Bernard, "Who Are the Japanese?" *Newsweek*, July 17, 1972, pp. 12–13.

6. Hida, Keiko, Shizue Nomoto and Midori Shigeta. "Family Com-

munication." Research Project, International Christian University, 1968.

7. Kaihara, Miwako. "A Comparative Study of Selected Communication Patterns in Japan and Costa Rica." Senior Thesis, International Christian University, 1972.

8. Ishikawa, Hiroyoshi, "Father is Complicated Person," *Japan Times*, January 1, 1973.

9. As quoted in Rudofsky, Bernard. *The Kimono Mind*. Tokyo: Tuttle, 1971, p. 157.

10. Kato, Hidetoshi. "Mutual Images: Japan and the United States Look at Each Other." Paper presented at the Conference on Intercultural Communication, International Christian University, 1972.

5.   Nonverbal Self Disclosure

1. Montagu, Ashley. *Touching: The Human Significance of the Skin*. New York: Harper & Row, 1971, p. 3.

2. Caudill, William and David Plath, "Who Sleeps by Whom? Parent-Child Involvement in Urban Japanese Families," *Psychiatry*, 26, 1966.

3. Dore, R. P. *City Life in Japan*. Berkeley: University of California Press, 1971.

4. Caudill, William and Helen Weinstein, "Maternal Care and Infant Behavior in Japan and America," *Psychiatry*, 32, 1969.

5. Jourard, Sidney, "An Exploratory Study of Body Accessibility," *British Journal of Social and Clinical Psychology*, 5, 1966.

6. Frank, Lawrence, "Tactile Communication, "*Genetic Psychology Monographs*, 56, 1957, p. 242.

6.   Defense Against Disclosure of Self

1. The impact of this fact can be seen in the study of decision-making. See Barnlund, Dean. "A Comparative Study of Individual, Majority and Group Decision-Making," *Journal of Abnormal and Social Psychology*, 58, 1959.

2. Barnlund, Dean, "Communication: The Context of Change," in Carl Larson and Frank Dance (Eds.), *Perspectives on Communication*, Milwaukee: University of Wisconsin, 1968.

3. Maraini, Fosco. *Japan: Patterns of Continuity*. Tokyo: Kodansha International, 1971, p. 191.

4. Halloran, *op. cit.*, p. 231.

5. Maraini, Fosco. *Meeting with Japan*. New York: Viking Press, 1960, p. 249.

6. Nitobe, Inazo. *Bushido, The Soul of Japan*. New York: Scribner's, 1931, p. 107.

7. Bairy, Maurice, "Japanese Ways," in Robert Ballon (Ed.), *Doing Business in Japan*, Tokyo: Tuttle, 1967, p. 24.

8. Ueda, Keiko. "Sixteen Different Ways to Avoid Saying 'No' in Japan."

Paper presented at the Conference on Intercultural Communication, International Christian University, 1972.

9. Nakano, Yuko. "How Japanese People Express Negative Feelings." Research Project, International Christian University, 1972.

10. Richie, *op. cit.*, p. 28.

7. Reflections

1. Benedict, *op. cit.*, p. 13.

2. Hall, Edward. *The Silent Language*. Garden City: Doubleday, 1959, p. 46.

3. Kawasaki, Ichiro. *Japan Unmasked*. Tokyo: Tuttle, 1969.

4. Abate and Berrien, *op. cit.*

5. Goffman, Erving. *Encounters: Two Studies in the Sociology of Interaction*. Indianapolis: Bobbs-Merrill, 1961, p. 41.

6. Jourard, *op. cit.*

7. The research on a number of the issues explored in this chapter can be reviewed in Barnlund, Dean. *Interpersonal Communication: Survey and Studies*. Boston: Houghton Mifflin, 1968.

8. As quoted by Liberman, *op. cit.*, p. 115.

9. Ikeda, Kiyoshi, "An Examination of Japanese English." *This Is Japan*, Tokyo: Asahi Shimbun Publishing Company, 1968, p. 100.

10. Wolff, K. *The Sociology of Georg Simmel*. New York: Free Press, 1964.

11. Steiner, George, as quoted in John Sisk, "On Being an Object," *Harper's Magazine*, 1974, p. 63.

12. Doi, Takeo, "Amae: A Key Concept for Understanding Japanese Personality Structure," in Robert Smith and Richard Beardsley (Eds.), *Japanese Culture: Its Development and Characteristics*, Chicago: Aldine, 1962, p. 133.

13. *Ibid.*, p. 138.

14. Jourard, *op. cit.*, p. 25.

15. Cozby, Paul, "Self-Disclosure: A Literature Review," *Psychological Bulletin*, 78, 1973, p. 78.

16. Jourard, *op. cit.*, p. iii.

17. Kirkup, James. *These Horned Islands*. New York: Macmillan, 1962, p. 411.

18. Maraini, Fosco, *Meeting with Japan*, op. cit., p. 98.

19. De Tocqueville, *op. cit.*, p. 192.

20. Larrabee, Eric. *The Self-Conscious Society*. Garden City: Doubleday, 1960, pp. 35–6.

21. Reston, James, Editorial, *San Francisco Chronicle*, April 28, 1974, p. 3.

22. De Tocqueville, *op. cit.*, p. 303.

23. Slater, Philip. *The Pursuit of Loneliness*. New York: Beacon, 1971, p. 7.

24. Eisenstadt, S.N., in Joseph *op. cit.*, p. 162.

25. Benedict, *op. cit.*, p. 315.

APPENDIX

Facts, in a sense, are inexhaustible. They can be viewed from an endless number of perspectives. Each in turn exposes another facet of reality. Some classic studies, completed decades ago, continue to stimulate new hypotheses, new research tools, and new theories bacause the raw data they generated were incorporated into their reports. Later it was possible to compare original findings with subsequent ones, or to compare them with data arising from alternative approaches to the same sort of events.

To encourage other analyses and to permit comparisons with other findings, a number of tables reporting the raw data obtained in this study have been reproduced in the following pages. These report the precise scores obtained from the Role Description Checklist, the Verbal Self Disclosure Scale, the Nonverbal Inventory, and the Defensive Strategy Scale. In nearly every case the findings have been organized and tabled to emphasize certain variables. Alternative groupings, however, can easily be set up. Here the focus is on comparisons between the two cultures, the two sexes, communicative associates, and various topics of conversation.

The reader may wish to use these tables in a number of different ways. One is simply to scan them searching for further patterns that may be of interest. Another is to look up precise scores obtained on a specific topic of conversation, an area of physical contact, or a particular defensive strategy. What appear to be relatively cold, lifeless, confusing series of numbers can, if examined carefully and creatively, yield an excitement of their own.

Culture Profiles

● Culture Profiles : Japan, United States

Interpersonal Characteristics	Japan		United States		Composite	
	Japanese Subjects	American Subjects	Japanese Subjects	American Subjects	Japan	United States
Formal	65	26	2	0	91	2
Independent	1	0	37	14	1	51
Talkative	3	1	50	17	4	67
Close	3	1	34	0	4	34
Shallow	7	7	14	6	14	20
Serious	45	9	2	3	54	5
Dependent	30	8	0	1	38	1
Calculating	11	4	9	3	15	12
Warm	14	4	9	4	18	13
Tense	21	9	1	0	30	1
Reserved	98	27	0	0	125	0
Frank	3	1	75	22	4	97
Trusting	6	3	0	1	9	1
Competitive	10	4	7	11	14	18
Masculine	0	1	10	1	1	11
Spontaneous	4	1	60	17	5	77

Open	2	0	22	10	2	32
Impulsive	2	3	18	14	5	32
Cool	3	5	7	1	8	8
To seek a protective relationship	20	9	3	0	29	3
Relaxed	5	1	31	10	6	41
Evasive	45	17	2	1	62	3
Silent	57	4	0	0	61	0
Self Assertive	4	1	75	24	5	99
Informal	5	3	58	20	8	78
Distant	32	6	4	4	38	8
Deep	13	3	0	1	16	1
Suspicious	3	4	2	1	7	3
Humorous	1	4	47	11	5	58
Cautious	47	21	2	2	68	4
Indifferent	14	2	5	4	16	9
Cooperative	11	14	1	18	25	19
Feminine	10	2	1	1	12	2
Responsive	15	5	5	5	20	10
Total	610	210	593	227	820	820

† Japanese Sample: N=122   American Sample: N=42   Total: N=164

● Verbal Disclosure : Japan & United States

							Target Persons							
	Stranger		Father		Mother		Same Sex Friend		Opposite Sex Friend		Untrusted Person		Topical Area Totals	
Topics	J†	A†	J	A	J	A	J	A	J	A	J	A	J	A
OPINIONS														
1. Religion	43	92	96	156	110	185	175	216	138	205	30	57	592	911
2. Communism	52	85	103	146	100	147	169	161	132	151	38	60	594	750
3. Integration	56	114	99	198	109	207	168	212	150	209	51	78	633	1018
4. Sex Standards	33	82	47	116	80	129	164	227	141	218	25	55	490	827
5. Social Standards	48	79	95	148	134	166	179	218	178	204	36	59	670	874
Total	232	452	440	764	533	834	855	1034	739	987	180	309	2979	4380
INTERESTS/TASTES														
1. Food	92	119	154	209	209	226	182	212	171	209	88	103	896	1078
2. Music	90	146	100	162	115	173	194	227	184	220	70	116	753	1044
3. Reading	83	117	95	158	103	171	202	201	180	201	61	95	724	943
4. TV and Movies	84	130	93	174	122	186	185	210	161	205	73	110	718	1015
5. Parties	48	91	99	153	127	165	182	229	157	224	30	74	643	936
Total	397	603	541	856	676	921	945	1079	853	1059	322	498	3734	5016

WORK/STUDIES														
1. Handicaps	26	59	101	166	145	184	163	205	142	196	14	19	591	829
2. Assets	25	75	116	174	141	185	156	197	130	191	16	46	584	868
3. Ambitions	32	107	113	187	129	199	162	211	144	212	21	60	601	976
4. Career Choice	32	102	115	187	140	200	168	210	140	206	18	58	613	963
5. Associates	21	74	94	188	127	195	162	206	131	199	13	27	548	889
Total	136	417	539	902	682	963	811	1029	687	1004	82	210	2937	4525
FINANCIAL														
1. Income	29	54	134	216	156	219	140	192	119	177	24	38	602	896
2. Debt	13	39	92	169	125	170	106	159	93	158	12	15	441	710
3. Savings	8	26	114	193	139	193	89	135	79	139	8	12	437	698
4. Needs	14	54	121	179	166	193	110	169	96	163	10	26	517	784
5. Budget	13	40	86	155	134	160	57	149	45	143	13	25	450	672
Total	77	213	547	912	720	935	547	804	489	780	67	116	2447	3760
PERSONALITY														
1. Handicaps	22	49	100	134	144	158	166	199	157	194	22	18	611	752
2. Self Control	16	47	79	117	122	146	173	191	136	197	14	15	540	713
3. Sex Life	4	16	21	51	43	65	111	170	76	179	4	4	259	485
4. Guilt/Shame	8	20	50	92	84	107	132	159	104	160	6	4	384	542
5. Pride	19	81	99	188	129	197	129	203	121	205	15	59	512	933
Total	69	213	349	582	522	673	711	922	594	935	61	100	2306	3425
PHYSICAL														
1. Facial	15	36	54	128	106	157	106	163	72	155	16	25	369	664
2. Appearance	15	23	47	95	93	121	99	140	71	127	17	24	342	530
3. Adequacy	10	29	45	106	104	143	114	168	71	152	14	24	358	622
4. Illness	19	71	110	173	141	190	119	176	92	167	25	45	506	822
5. Sex Adequacy	3	23	30	28	40	38	96	136	59	158	5	15	233	398
Total	62	182	286	530	484	649	534	783	365	759	77	133	1808	3036

| Target Person Totals | 973 | 2080 | 2702 | 4546 | 3617 | 4965 | 4403 | 5651 | 3727 | 5524 | 789 | 1366 | 16211 | 24142 |

† J=Japanese A=Americans N (Japanese)=120 (60 Males, 60 Females) N (Americans)=120 (60 Males, 60 Females)

● Verbal Disclosure : Japanese Males & Females

							Target Persons							
Topics	Stranger		Father		Mother		Same Sex Friend		Opposite Sex Friend		Untrusted Person		Topical Area Totals	
	M†	F†	M	F	M	F	M	F	M	F	M	F	M	F
OPINIONS														
1. Religion	23	20	46	50	49	61	85	90	71	67	20	10	284	299
2. Communism	32	20	58	45	55	45	98	71	63	69	25	13	331	263
3. Integration	33	23	52	47	52	57	93	75	75	75	34	17	339	294
4. Sex Standards	23	10	28	19	33	47	83	81	71	70	18	7	256	234
5. Social Standards	27	21	48	47	57	77	84	95	77	101	26	10	319	351
Total	138	94	232	208	246	287	433	412	357	382	123	57	1539	1440
INTERESTS/TASTES														
1. Food	47	45	74	80	103	106	78	104	84	87	45	43	431	465
2. Music	43	47	42	58	51	64	99	95	93	91	39	31	367	386
3. Reading	47	36	46	49	46	57	101	101	87	93	38	23	365	359
4. TV and Movies	38	46	44	49	56	66	91	94	81	80	39	34	349	369
5. Parties	31	17	55	44	63	64	96	86	81	76	20	10	346	297
Total	206	191	261	280	319	357	465	480	426	427	181	141	1858	1876
WORK/STUDIES														
1. Handicaps	17	9	58	43	66	79	73	90	66	76	9	5	289	302
2. Assets	16	9	58	58	65	76	81	75	63	67	11	5	294	290
3. Ambitions	16	16	52	61	60	69	79	83	70	74	12	9	289	312
4. Career Choice	18	14	57	58	65	75	83	85	62	78	10	8	295	318

5. Associates	12	9	48	46	60	67	83	79	64	67	7	6	274	274
Total	79	57	273	266	316	266	399	412	325	362	49	33	1441	1496
FINANCIAL														
1. Income	16	13	69	65	68	88	72	68	56	63	14	10	295	307
2. Debt	9	4	47	45	62	63	59	47	48	45	9	3	234	207
3. Savings	7	1	55	59	64	75	53	36	41	38	6	2	226	211
4. Needs	10	4	58	63	76	90	66	44	56	40	8	2	274	243
5. Budget	9	4	41	45	62	72	57	45	40	62	9	4	218	232
Total	51	26	270	277	332	388	307	240	241	248	46	21	1247	1200
PERSONALITY														
1. Handicaps	11	11	50	50	67	77	87	79	73	84	12	10	300	311
2. Self Control	13	3	39	40	57	65	86	87	66	70	8	6	269	271
3. Sex Life	4	0	14	7	22	21	74	37	37	39	4	0	155	104
4. Guilt/Shame	5	3	32	18	39	45	71	61	52	52	4	2	203	181
5. Pride	13	6	46	53	61	68	68	61	64	57	12	3	264	248
Total	46	23	181	168	246	276	386	325	292	302	40	21	1191	1115
PHYSICAL														
1. Facial	8	7	17	37	37	69	42	64	29	43	8	8	141	228
2. Appearance	6	9	19	28	33	60	39	60	31	40	9	8	137	205
3. Adequacy	7	3	24	21	37	67	46	68	34	37	9	5	157	201
4. Illness	12	7	57	53	57	84	60	59	47	45	19	6	252	254
5. Sex Adequacy	3	0	17	13	19	21	62	34	37	22	5	0	143	90
Total	36	26	134	152	183	301	249	285	178	187	50	27	830	978
Target Person Totals	556	417	1351	1351	1642	1975	2239	2154	1819	1908	489	300	8106	8105

† M=Males   F=Females   N (Males)=60   N (Females)=60

Verbal Disclosure : American Males & Females

							Target Persons							
	Stranger		Father		Mother		Same Sex Friend		Opposite Sex Friend		Untrusted Person		Topical Area Totals	
Topics	M†	F†	M	F	M	F	M	F	M	F	M	F	M	F
OPINIONS														
1. Religion	49	43	82	74	95	90	110	106	106	99	31	26	473	438
2. Communism	50	35	80	66	80	67	91	70	82	69	34	26	417	433
3. Integration	62	52	99	99	102	105	111	101	108	101	47	31	529	489
4. Sex Standards	44	38	61	55	58	71	113	114	107	111	29	26	412	415
5. Social Standards	36	43	75	73	73	93	108	110	104	100	28	31	424	450
Total	241	211	397	367	408	426	533	501	507	480	169	140	2255	2125
INTERESTS/TASTES														
1. Food	60	59	109	100	113	113	103	109	105	104	50	53	540	538
2. Music	76	70	80	82	81	92	116	111	113	107	63	53	529	515
3. Reading	55	62	80	78	83	88	96	105	99	102	47	48	460	483
4. TV and Movies	70	60	88	86	89	97	108	102	101	104	60	50	516	499
5. Parties	52	39	74	79	76	89	116	113	113	111	42	32	473	462
Total	313	290	431	425	442	479	539	540	531	528	262	236	2578	2498
WORK/STUDIES														
1. Handicaps	30	29	86	80	88	96	98	107	93	103	8	11	403	426
2. Assets	44	31	92	82	93	92	103	94	100	91	23	23	455	413
3. Ambitions	57	50	101	86	101	98	107	104	108	104	30	30	504	472
4. Career Choice	51	51	101	86	103	97	108	102	104	102	29	29	496	467
5. Associates	43	31	97	91	94	101	105	101	103	96	14	13	456	433
Total	225	192	477	425	479	484	521	508	508	496	104	106	2314	2211
FINANCIAL														
1. Income	31	23	113	103	112	107	100	92	94	83	20	18	470	426
2. Debt	22	17	87	82	86	84	84	75	79	79	4	11	362	348

3. Savings	14	12	103	90	105	88	73	62	77	62	3	9	375	323
4. Needs	34	20	97	82	97	96	86	83	81	82	9	17	404	380
5. Budget	26	14	83	72	82	78	78	71	77	66	11	14	357	315
Total	127	86	483	429	482	453	421	383	408	372	47	69	1968	1792
PERSONALITY														
1. Handicaps	30	19	70	64	75	83	92	107	95	99	9	9	371	381
2. Self Control	28	19	59	58	64	82	91	100	98	99	7	8	347	366
3. Sex Life	11	5	30	21	26	39	82	88	87	92	2	2	238	247
4. Guilt/Shame	12	8	51	41	50	57	74	85	76	84	0	4	263	279
5. Pride	52	29	98	90	100	97	106	97	107	98	36	23	499	434
Total	133	80	308	274	315	358	445	477	463	472	54	46	1718	1707
PHYSICAL														
1. Facial	20	16	60	68	63	94	69	94	75	80	12	13	299	366
2. Appearance	13	10	42	53	43	78	55	85	62	65	12	12	227	303
3. Adequacy	21	8	56	50	56	87	68	100	71	81	16	8	288	334
4. Illness	38	33	93	80	96	94	89	87	86	81	24	21	426	396
5. Sex Adequacy	19	4	23	5	21	17	70	66	81	77	10	5	224	174
Total	111	71	274	256	279	370	351	432	375	384	74	59	1464	1572
Target Person Totals	1150	930	2370	2176	2405	2570	2810	2841	2792	2730	710	656	12237	11905

† M=Males   F=Females   N (Males)=60   N (Females)=60

Physical Contact

Physical Contact: Japan & United States (Parents)

Body Region*	Touching				Touched by				Totals				Total Parent Contact	
	Mother		Father		Mother		Father		Mother		Father			
	J	A	J	A	J	A	J	A	J	A	J	A	J	A
1	76	96	41	92	95	111	64	100	171	207	105	192	276	399
2	28	59	10	47	39	73	12	52	67	132	22	99	89	231
3	27	59	22	56	50	70	20	57	77	129	42	113	119	242
4	29	56	13	51	37	66	14	53	66	122	27	104	93	226
5	27	87	14	61	37	92	15	66	64	179	29	127	93	306
6	52	75	32	62	45	75	27	62	97	150	59	124	156	274
7	65	64	45	72	55	78	35	63	120	142	80	135	200	277
8	15	17	11	39	20	44	10	26	35	61	21	65	56	126
9	20	46	10	55	25	55	7	43	45	101	17	98	62	199
10	11	10	2	6	17	17	4	9	28	27	6	15	34	42
11	14	42	9	32	20	42	7	35	34	84	16	67	50	151
12	23	42	17	37	32	47	13	44	55	89	30	81	85	170
13	28	35	22	30	37	39	14	31	65	74	36	61	101	135
14	33	46	22	39	34	58	16	47	67	104	38	86	105	190
15	57	92	41	84	56	89	34	81	113	181	75	165	188	346

16	64	87	50	81	56	83	37	79	120	170	87	160	207	330
17	81	98	66	98	84	100	68	100	165	198	134	198	299	396
18	60	80	39	66	63	85	45	81	123	165	84	147	207	312
19	69	73	52	59	62	72	40	69	131	145	92	128	223	273
20	81	87	69	87	71	86	54	86	152	173	123	173	275	346
21	54	76	35	66	49	80	28	72	103	156	63	138	166	294
22	17	33	5	23	21	46	5	31	38	79	10	54	48	133
23	11	27	6	21	15	26	4	26	26	53	10	47	36	100
24	19	28	13	25	20	31	10	28	39	59	23	53	62	112
Total	961	1415	646	1289	1040	1565	583	1341	2001	2980	1229	2630	3230	5610

† N (Japanese)=120 (60 Males, 60 Females)   N (Americans)=120 (60 Males, 60 Females)   Total N=240   * See Chapter 5, p. 99, Figure 13.

● Physical Contact: Japan & United States (Friends)

Body Region*	Touching				Touched by				Totals					
	Opposite Sex Friend		Same Sex Friend		Opposite Sex Friend		Same Sex Friend		Opposite Sex Friend		Same Sex Friend		Total Peer Contact	
	J	A	J	A	J	A	J	A	J	A	J	A	J	A
1	82	111	79	82	79	112	85	83	161	223	164	165	325	388
2	29	99	17	48	36	102	23	48	65	201	40	96	105	297
3	49	110	25	50	54	109	31	49	103	219	56	99	159	318
4	45	105	19	47	46	106	23	48	91	211	42	95	133	306
5	60	116	20	61	63	116	24	60	123	232	44	121	167	353
6	50	109	34	60	59	111	39	56	109	220	73	116	182	336
7	66	109	65	71	69	108	64	69	135	217	129	140	264	357
8	44	106	16	35	39	106	17	36	83	212	33	71	116	283
9	38	107	19	50	40	107	17	47	78	214	36	97	114	311
10	28	96	5	14	28	96	8	15	56	192	13	29	69	221
11	31	103	21	46	35	101	23	46	66	204	44	92	110	296
12	32	97	31	43	35	94	35	42	67	191	66	85	133	276

Body Region	Touching Mother J/M	Touching Mother J/F	Touching Father J/M	Touching Father J/F	Touched by Mother J/M	Touched by Mother J/F	Touched by Father J/M	Touched by Father J/F	Totals Mother J/M	Totals Mother J/F	Totals Father J/M	Totals Father J/F	Total Parent Contact J/M	Total Parent Contact J/F
13	27	90	32	35	34	89	33	36	61	178	65	71	126	250
14	29	91	30	43	34	92	30	47	63	183	60	90	123	273
15	64	114	73	84	68	110	72	89	132	224	145	173	277	397
16	76	111	81	92	79	111	87	93	155	222	168	185	323	407
17	91	113	99	94	101	112	98	91	192	225	197	185	389	410
18	69	105	61	75	67	105	66	79	136	210	127	154	263	364
19	56	103	48	68	66	108	50	70	122	211	98	138	220	349
20	86	108	85	92	84	110	90	91	170	218	175	183	345	401
21	64	108	48	69	67	108	54	72	131	216	102	141	233	357
22	29	101	20	39	30	102	24	38	59	203	44	77	103	280
23	24	85	13	29	20	87	17	33	44	172	30	62	74	234
24	19	86	22	31	27	88	22	30	46	174	44	61	90	235
Total	1188	2483	963	1358	1260	2490	1032	1368	2448	4973	1995	2726	4443	7699

† N (Japanese) = 120 (60 Males, 60 Females) N (Americans) = 120 (60 Males, 60 Females) Total N=240 * See Chapter 5, p. 99, Figure 13.

● Physical Contact: Japanese Males & Females (Parents)

Body Region*	Touching Mother J/M	Touching Mother J/F	Touching Father J/M	Touching Father J/F	Touched by Mother J/M	Touched by Mother J/F	Touched by Father J/M	Touched by Father J/F	Totals Mother J/M	Totals Mother J/F	Totals Father J/M	Totals Father J/F	Total Parent Contact J/M	Total Parent Contact J/F
1	31	45	18	23	43	52	33	31	74	97	51	54	125	151
2	7	21	3	7	17	22	7	5	24	43	10	12	34	55
3	7	20	8	14	23	27	11	9	30	47	19	23	49	70
4	9	20	5	8	14	23	4	10	23	43	9	18	32	61
5	9	18	6	8	12	25	6	9	21	43	12	17	33	60
6	22	30	14	18	19	26	12	15	41	56	26	33	67	89
7	24	41	22	23	25	30	23	12	49	71	45	35	94	106
8	3	12	5	6	11	9	8	2	14	21	13	8	27	29
9	5	15	4	6	10	15	4	3	15	20	8	9	23	39

Region														
10	5	6	1	1	7	10	4	0	12	16	5	1	17	17
11	3	11	5	4	4	16	2	5	7	27	7	9	14	36
12	4	19	6	11	8	24	5	8	12	43	11	19	23	62
13	5	23	6	16	10	27	6	8	15	50	12	24	27	74
14	13	20	9	13	14	20	7	9	27	40	16	22	43	62
15	18	39	15	26	19	37	14	20	37	76	29	46	66	122
16	20	44	18	32	19	37	13	24	39	81	31	56	70	137
17	35	46	32	34	37	47	34	34	72	93	66	68	138	161
18	22	38	15	24	23	40	21	24	45	78	36	48	81	126
19	27	42	24	28	27	35	20	20	54	77	44	48	98	125
20	33	48	36	33	29	42	29	25	62	90	65	58	127	148
21	16	38	15	20	13	36	11	17	29	74	26	37	55	111
22	4	13	2	3	5	16	3	2	9	29	5	5	14	34
23	3	8	3	3	3	12	2	2	6	20	5	5	11	25
24	6	13	4	9	6	14	3	7	12	27	7	16	19	43
Total	331	630	276	370	398	642	282	301	729	1272	558	671	1287	1943

† J/M = Japanese Males   J/F = Japanese Females   N (Males) = 60   N (Females) = 60   Total N = 120   * See Chapter 5, p. 99, Figure 13.

● Physical Contact: Japanese Males & Females (Friends)

Body Region*	Touching				Touched by				Totals				Total Peer Contact	
	Opposite Sex Friend		Same Sex Friend		Opposite Sex Friend		Same Sex Friend		Opposite Sex Friend		Same Sex Friend			
	J/M	J/F	J/M	J/F	J/M	J/F	J/M	J/F	J/M	J/F	J/M	J/F	J/M	J/F
1	38	44	34	45	33	46	40	45	71	90	74	89	145	179
2	13	16	3	14	13	23	7	16	26	39	10	30	36	69
3	22	27	6	19	19	35	12	19	41	62	18	38	59	100
4	21	24	6	13	14	32	8	15	35	56	14	28	49	84
5	30	30	7	13	25	38	9	15	55	68	16	28	71	96
6	26	24	14	20	24	35	17	22	50	59	31	42	81	101

Body Region*	Touching				Touched by				Totals				Total Parent Contact	
	Mother A/M	Mother A/F	Father A/M	Father A/F	Mother A/M	Mother A/F	Father A/M	Father A/F	Mother A/M	Mother A/F	Father A/M	Father A/F	A/M	A/F
7	34	32	33	32	30	39	36	28	64	71	69	60	133	131
8	25	19	13	3	17	22	14	3	42	41	27	6	69	47
9	21	17	11	8	18	22	12	5	39	39	23	13	62	52
10	17	11	3	2	13	15	4	4	30	26	7	6	37	32
11	18	13	10	11	12	23	11	12	30	36	21	23	51	59
12	15	17	10	21	12	23	13	22	27	40	23	43	50	83
13	14	13	12	20	13	21	14	19	27	34	26	39	53	73
14	13	16	14	16	14	20	16	14	27	36	30	30	57	66
15	27	37	29	44	28	40	30	42	55	77	59	86	114	163
16	32	44	32	49	32	47	37	50	64	91	69	99	133	190
17	40	51	47	52	47	54	48	50	87	105	95	102	182	207
18	36	33	28	33	27	40	28	38	63	73	56	71	119	144
19	29	27	17	31	27	39	19	31	56	66	36	62	92	128
20	44	42	41	44	36	48	46	44	80	90	87	88	167	178
21	35	29	20	28	31	36	23	31	66	65	43	59	109	124
22	19	10	11	9	11	19	16	8	30	29	27	17	57	46
23	12	12	7	6	7	13	11	6	19	25	18	12	37	37
24	11	8	10	12	9	18	11	11	20	26	21	23	41	49
Total	592	596	418	545	512	748	482	550	1104	1344	900	1095	2004	2439

† N (Males)=60   N (Females)=60   Total N=120   See Chapter 5, p. 99, Figure 13.

● Physical Contact: American Males & Females (Parents)

Body Region*	Touching				Touched by				Totals				Total Parent Contact	
	Mother A/M	Mother A/F	Father A/M	Father A/F	Mother A/M	Mother A/F	Father A/M	Father A/F	Mother A/M	Mother A/F	Father A/M	Father A/F	A/M	A/F
1	43	53	45	47	56	55	48	52	99	108	93	99	192	207
2	21	38	20	27	35	38	24	28	56	76	44	55	100	131
3	24	35	21	35	33	37	25	32	57	72	46	67	103	139

Physical Contact: American Males & Females (Friends)

Body Region*	Touching				Touched by				Totals				Total Peer Contact	
	Opposite Sex Friend		Same Sex Friend		Opposite Sex Friend		Same Sex Friend		Opposite Sex Friend		Same Sex Friend			
	A/M	A/F	A/M	A/F	A/M	A/F	A/M	A/F	A/M	A/F	A/M	A/F	A/M	A/F
1	54	57	40	42	54	58	40	43	108	115	80	85	188	200
4	24	32	19	32	33	33	25	28	57	65	44	60	101	125
5	42	45	19	42	45	47	25	41	87	92	44	83	131	175
6	37	38	31	31	38	37	30	32	75	75	61	63	136	138
7	26	38	32	40	30	40	29	34	64	78	61	74	125	152
8	5	12	19	20	31	13	18	8	36	25	37	28	73	53
9	14	32	24	31	24	31	19	24	38	63	43	55	81	118
10	0	10	3	3	7	10	6	3	7	20	9	6	16	26
11	16	26	17	15	18	24	17	18	34	50	34	33	68	83
12	13	29	14	23	18	29	17	27	31	58	31	50	62	108
13	13	22	12	18	16	23	15	16	29	45	27	34	56	79
14	21	25	17	22	27	31	23	24	48	56	40	46	88	102
15	40	52	34	50	39	50	36	45	79	102	70	95	149	197
16	37	50	33	48	37	46	34	45	74	96	67	93	141	189
17	47	51	47	51	48	52	48	52	95	103	95	103	190	206
18	34	46	30	36	42	43	40	41	76	89	70	77	146	166
19	32	41	23	36	35	37	35	34	67	78	58	70	125	148
20	37	50	37	50	38	48	42	44	75	98	79	94	154	192
21	35	41	28	38	35	45	36	36	70	86	64	74	134	160
22	11	22	8	15	20	26	13	18	31	48	21	33	52	81
23	9	18	10	11	11	15	13	13	20	33	23	24	43	57
24	12	16	11	14	14	17	14	14	26	33	25	28	51	61
Total	593	822	554	735	738	827	632	709	1331	1649	1186	1444	2517	3093

† A/M=American Males A/F=American Females N (Males)=60 N(Females)=60 Total N=120 * See Chapter 5, p. 99, Figure 13.

2	47	52	23	25	48	54	23	25	95	106	46	50	141	156
3	53	57	24	26	53	56	23	26	106	113	47	52	153	165
4	51	54	20	27	52	54	23	25	103	108	43	52	146	160
5	56	60	24	37	56	60	23	37	112	120	47	74	159	194
6	53	56	29	31	53	58	26	30	106	114	55	61	161	175
7	54	55	38	33	53	55	37	32	107	110	75	65	182	175
8	52	54	27	8	52	54	28	8	104	108	55	16	159	124
9	50	57	27	23	50	57	25	22	100	114	52	45	152	159
10	49	47	10	4	44	52	9	6	93	99	19	10	112	109
11	52	51	24	22	48	53	25	21	100	104	49	43	149	147
12	48	49	21	22	46	48	19	23	94	97	40	45	134	142
13	47	43	17	18	45	44	18	18	92	87	35	36	127	123
14	43	48	17	26	44	48	23	24	87	96	40	50	127	146
15	55	59	39	45	53	57	42	47	108	116	81	92	189	208
16	53	58	41	51	52	59	41	52	105	117	82	103	187	220
17	53	60	46	48	54	58	44	47	107	118	90	95	197	213
18	52	53	33	42	52	53	35	44	104	106	68	86	172	192
19	48	55	30	38	50	58	32	38	98	113	62	76	160	189
20	54	54	45	47	54	56	44	47	108	110	89	94	197	204
21	54	51	35	34	52	56	36	36	106	110	71	70	177	180
22	50	51	24	15	46	56	24	14	96	107	48	29	144	136
23	44	41	17	12	45	42	19	14	89	83	36	26	125	109
24	44	42	16	15	45	43	16	14	89	85	32	29	121	114
Total	1216	1267	667	691	1201	1289	675	693	2417	2556	1342	1384	3759	3940

† N(Males)=60   N (Females)=60   Total N=120   * See Chapter 5, p. 99, Figure 13.

Defensive Strategy Scale

● Defensive Strategy Scale : Males & Females—Low & High Threat

TARGET PERSONS

Defensive Strategy Preference*		Total	Opposite Sex Friend	Same Sex Friend	Father	Mother	Stranger	Unrespected Person	Respected Person	Opposite Sex Associate	Same Sex Associate	Subordinate Person	Superior Person	Younger Person	Older Person
1	J	345	14	11	31	29	38	36	30	21	16	20	30	15	54
1	A	148	3	7	9	6	18	8	19	7	5	7	30	3	26
2	J	129	3	1	7	13	26	18	2	9	3	16	5	16	10
2	A	74	0	0	2	2	14	7	2	8	6	5	5	12	11
3	J	250	22	12	15	10	14	22	13	27	24	24	29	21	17
3	A	101	8	5	5	3	8	4	6	19	13	2	9	8	11

															Total
4	J	29	27	35	32	48	45	26	21	24	18	24	32	31	392
	A	19	9	16	11	15	17	10	2	13	6	9	7	6	141
5	J	16	18	15	17	14	13	9	12	9	10	8	7	11	159
	A	5	10	3	5	6	7	3	9	14	0	0	1	2	65
6	J	13	27	16	34	24	25	12	27	20	17	22	16	14	267
	A	3	8	7	11	3	11	4	4	5	6	6	1	2	71
7	J	35	17	30	20	11	16	8	17	14	10	16	7	7	208
	A	16	6	12	11	5	12	7	5	12	11	7	4	6	114
8	J	9	12	10	13	18	13	22	10	8	11	10	21	16	173
	A	4	2	5	2	5	1	11	1	2	1	4	2	2	42
9	J	17	42	19	30	38	24	28	45	39	51	46	46	51	476
	A	17	15	19	34	20	16	7	24	22	20	14	12	10	230
10	J	20	10	16	5	13	13	17	6	8	4	15	7	6	140
	A	11	7	36	4	9	13	13	2	7	18	23	7	11	161
11	J	12	8	25	6	12	7	56	3	9	35	25	65	43	306
	A	52	29	56	41	45	46	96	14	27	66	67	110	116	775
12	J	6	7	7	6	5	5	9	3	3	15	12	2	9	89
	A	44	39	35	43	58	48	54	31	34	80	83	67	62	678
13	J	2	14	3	14	11	19	8	9	11	7	2	8	12	120
	A	15	58	3	31	34	24	4	49	14	10	4	13	10	269
14	J	0	6	0	3	3	3	0	11	17	10	7	5	1	66
	A	6	34	4	33	16	11	4	80	50	11	7	4	2	262
Total	J	240	240	240	240	240	240	240	240	240	240	240	240	240	240
	A	240	240	240	240	240	240	240	240	240	240	240	240	240	240

† N(Japanese)=240   N(Americans)=240   Total N=480   * For a description of these defensive strategies, see Chapter 6, p. 118.

● Defensive Strategy Scale : Japanese Males & Females (Low & High Threat)

TARGET PERSONS

Defensive Strategy Preference*	M/F	Older Person	Younger Person	Superior Person	Subordinate Person	Same Sex Associate	Opposite Sex Associate	Respected Person	Unrespected Person	Stranger	Mother	Father	Same Sex Friend	Opposite Sex Friend	Total
1	M	24	8	12	11	9	11	15	22	16	16	15	8	6	173
	F	30	7	18	9	7	10	15	14	22	13	16	3	8	172
2	M	5	10	1	11	2	3	2	6	13	7	5	0	2	67
	F	5	6	4	5	1	6	0	12	13	6	2	1	1	62
3	M	9	8	15	8	9	14	10	8	7	4	7	5	10	114
	F	8	13	14	16	15	13	3	14	7	6	8	7	12	136
4	M	13	12	13	17	19	18	9	9	7	11	14	18	15	175
	F	16	15	22	15	29	27	17	12	17	7	10	14	16	217
5	M	13	12	14	11	8	11	9	8	5	8	8	7	9	123
	F	3	6	1	6	6	2	0	4	4	2	0	0	2	36
6	M	6	8	5	11	9	11	5	9	8	7	10	6	4	99
	F	7	19	11	23	15	14	7	18	12	10	12	10	10	168
7	M	14	10	18	12	8	10	5	11	10	6	6	5	5	120
	F	21	7	12	8	3	6	3	6	4	4	10	2	2	88

198

		1	2	3	4	5	6	7	8	9	10	11	12	13	Total
8	M	6	8	3	6	8	6	10	4	3	7	5	10	7	83
	F	3	4	7	7	10	7	12	6	5	4	5	11	9	90
9	M	10	20	12	14	24	10	14	27	21	21	22	20	21	236
	F	7	22	7	16	14	14	14	18	18	30	24	26	30	240
10	M	8	5	6	1	5	6	5	3	3	1	6	2	2	53
	F	12	5	10	4	8	7	12	3	5	3	9	5	4	87
11	M	7	4	13	3	6	3	29	3	7	15	11	27	22	150
	F	5	4	12	3	6	4	27	0	2	20	14	38	21	156
12	M	4	5	5	5	4	3	4	1	3	7	7	0	6	54
	F	2	2	2	1	1	2	5	2	0	8	5	2	3	35
13	M	1	6	3	9	7	12	3	3	5	5	2	7	11	74
	F	1	8	0	5	4	7	5	6	6	2	0	1	1	46
14	M	0	4	0	1	2	2	0	6	12	5	2	5	0	39
	F	0	2	0	2	1	1	0	5	5	5	5	0	1	27
Total	M	120	120	120	120	120	120	120	120	120	120	120	120	120	120
	F	120	120	120	120	120	120	120	120	120	120	120	120	120	120

† N (Males)=120   N (Females)=120   Total N=240   * For a description of these defensive strategies, see Chapter 6, p. 118.

Defensive Strategy Scale : American Males & Females (Low & High Threat)

TARGET PERSONS

Defensive Strategy Preference*		Total	Opposite Sex Friend	Same Sex Friend	Father	Mother	Stranger	Unrespected Person	Respected Person	Opposite Sex Associate	Same Sex Associate	Subordinate Person	Superior Person	Younger Person	Older Person
1	M	77	2	5	7	4	10	2	9	2	2	3	12	2	17
1	F	71	1	2	2	2	8	6	10	5	3	4	18	1	9
2	M	37	0	0	1	2	6	1	2	4	5	3	4	5	4
2	F	37	0	0	1	0	8	6	0	4	1	2	1	7	7
3	M	56	4	4	4	3	4	2	3	10	5	1	6	3	5
3	F	45	4	1	1	0	4	2	3	9	8	1	3	3	6
4	M	71	3	3	4	2	9	2	4	8	10	6	7	3	10
4	F	69	3	4	5	4	4	0	6	9	5	5	9	6	9
5	M	29	1	1	0	0	7	5	1	3	1	2	1	5	2
5	F	36	1	0	0	0	7	4	2	4	5	3	2	5	3
6	M	36	1	1	3	2	2	0	3	9	2	4	5	3	1
6	F	35	1	0	3	4	3	4	1	2	1	7	2	5	2
7	M	80	4	3	5	7	8	4	3	9	5	8	10	4	10
7	F	34	2	1	2	4	4	1	4	3	0	3	2	2	6

															Total
8	M	2	0	4	0	2	1	7	0	0	0	0	1	2	19
	F	2	2	1	2	3	0	4	1	2	1	4	1	0	23
9	M	6	8	8	15	7	5	5	6	8	12	7	4	5	96
	F	11	7	11	19	13	11	2	18	14	8	7	8	5	134
10	M	6	2	20	2	1	4	5	1	3	12	14	2	4	76
	F	5	5	16	2	8	9	8	1	4	6	9	5	7	85
11	M	19	10	18	15	19	21	47	7	6	32	35	50	57	336
	F	33	19	38	26	26	25	49	7	21	34	32	60	59	429
12	M	23	22	18	16	25	21	27	17	15	31	32	34	28	309
	F	21	17	17	27	33	27	27	14	19	49	51	33	34	369
13	M	10	34	3	24	25	17	2	24	11	6	4	8	7	175
	F	5	24	0	7	9	7	2	25	3	4	0	5	3	94
14	M	5	17	4	21	11	6	2	49	31	7	4	4	2	163
	F	1	17	0	12	5	5	2	31	19	4	3	0	0	99
Total	M	120	120	120	120	120	120	120	120	120	120	120	120	120	120
	F	120	120	120	120	120	120	120	120	120	120	120	120	120	120

† N (Males) = 120   N (Females) = 120   Total N = 240   * For a description of these defensive strategies, see Chapter 6, p. 118.